SYMPHONIC REPERTOIRE for PERCUSSION ACCESSORIES

*Tambourine, Triangle, Bass Drum, Castanets, Maracas,
Concert Toms, and Roto Toms*

Tim Genis

Edited by Anthony J. Cirone

Published by
Meredith Music Publications
a division of G.W. Music, Inc.
4899 Lerch Creek Ct., Galesville, MD 20765
http://www.meredithmusic.com

MEREDITH MUSIC PUBLICATIONS and its stylized double M logo are trademarks of
MEREDITH MUSIC PUBLICATIONS, a division of G.W. Music, Inc.

Cover designer: Shawn Girsberger
Text Editor: Josie Cirone

No part of this book may be reproduced or transmitted in any form or by any means, electronic or
mechanical, including photocopying, recording, or by any informational storage or retrieval system
without permission in writing from the publisher.

Copyright © 2009 MEREDITH MUSIC PUBLICATIONS
International Copyright Secured • All Rights Reserved
First Edition
October 2009

International Standard Book Number: 978-1-57463-110-4
Printed and bound in U.S.A.

D1611510

Foreword

As a timpanist, the thought of writing a book on percussion accessory instruments seemed a bit daunting; but, it also stirred excitement in me since I would be able to share insights I've gathered over the years. I have always been enthusiastic when given a part I could interpret. I share my ideas in this book, giving the reader a broader scope for expanding his or her repertoire of techniques for creating different colors. I would, however, find it limiting if the readers took these suggestions at face value rather than building them into their own repertory of techniques.

The historical significance of some instruments made a difference in my approach to the excerpts; for instance, Arabic vs. Southern Italian tambourine playing produces two different results and Orchestral vs. Ethnic Techniques leave two contrasting impressions. In short, having a broad range of knowledge and playing styles results in a well-rounded, creative player—one who inflects more subtleties and colors into a performance.

Adding certain articulations to a non-sustaining instrument might be confusing to some readers. A tambourine, for instance, is regarded as an instrument that cannot produce a long tone with a single stroke. Although it does not have the sustaining quality similar to a triangle or cymbal, it can clearly create a short staccato sound vs. a longer tenuto articulation. This is achieved with stroke speed and by allowing the jingles to resonate (holding the tambourine in a vertical position). To play a very short note, the tambourine is held flat (parallel to the ground), and struck with a very quick wristy motion. Conversely, if a long "sustained" note is desired, the stroke is slowed down and the tambourine angled so the jingles are looser, providing a bit more ring. There are tricks to altering articulation and it is a challenge and joy to explore the possibilities.

The orchestral percussionist's job has grown to new levels of artistic challenges. I remember Roland Kohloff, my former teacher, saying: "The bar will continue to keep rising to higher and higher levels." The joy of musical expression is very personal and communicated in different ways—the possibilities are endless.

It is my hope that all who read this book will gather new insights and have as much fun performing the excerpts as I had interpreting them. Enjoy!

Tim Genis

Contents

Tambourine

Tambourine Techniques 4

Carmen Suites, No. 1 & No. 2—George Bizet 5

Carnival Overture—Antonín Dvořák 10

Peter Grimes, Storm Scene—Benjamin Britten 15

Petrouchka—Igor Stravinsky 18

Polovetsian Dances—Alexander Borodin 20

Roman Carnival Overture—Hector Berlioz 26

Scheherazade—N. Rimsky-Korsakow 29

Triangle

Symphony No. 4, Movement III—Johannes Brahms.........................33

Capriccio Espagnol, I & II. Alborado—N. Rimsky Korsakov..............35

Piano Concerto, No. 1—Franz Liszt...39

Sheherazade, Movement II, III, IV—N. Rimsky-Korsakow................42

Bass Drum

The Rite of Spring—Igor Stravinsky 48

Symphony No. 3, Movements I, III, VI—Gustav Mahler 57

Castanets

Capriccio Espagnol, V. Fandango asturiano—N. Rimsky Korsakow.............66

Maracas

Cuban Overture—George Gershwin 68

Concert Tom Toms

Symphonic Dances from "West Side Story"—Leonard Bernstein.................72

Roto-Toms

The Rose Lake—Michael Tippett 75

About the Author..80

❦

Tambourine Techniques

Some of the tambourine techniques used in the following pieces need a detailed explanation; therefore, I have outlined them and will refer to them by title as they come up.

Open—Hand Thumb Roll

This is a standard thumb roll. Position the hand as if to wave at someone. Place the thumb near the bottom of the tambourine, close to the holding hand. With a rounded thumb, press along the edge of the tambourine to produce close bounces.

The other fingers should be in the wave position, ready to pivot the hand over to articulate the end of the roll—or, snap the heel of the hand onto the head to achieve the same result.

Braced Third-Finger Roll

This method is the same as a thumb roll; but, instead of using the thumb to produce a roll, use the third finger. Brace the finger with the thumb and execute the bounces in the same way as for a thumb roll.

Un-Braced Third-Finger Roll

The hand position for this roll can be realized by placing the hand in the braced third-finger position. Then move the thumb away from the third finger (1-½ inches). This is the desired hand position. Execute the roll with the third finger. The thumb is now in the ready position to articulate the end of a roll.

Standard Shake Roll

Execute this roll with the holding hand. The tambourine is pivoted by the wrist, using the same motion as if turning a doorknob.

Assisted Shake Roll

This technique is effective for starting a very soft roll. Hold the tambourine about three feet above the ground and place the tips of the third and fourth fingers of the striking hand against the edge of the tambourine (just below the holding hand). Jostle the striking hand in a quick vibrating motion. Practice a smooth transition from the Assisted Shake Roll into the Standard Shake Roll.

Knee-Fist Method

This method is executed by placing the foot on the edge of a chair and turning the tambourine over so the head is facing the top of the knee. Strike the tambourine with the fist on the inside of the tambourine and the knee on the outside of the head.

From Carmen Suites - No. 1. & No. 2.

Georges Bizet

No. 1. Aragonaise

Tambourine

1. Opening Eighteen Measures:
   Begin the opening eighteen measures with the fist striking the center of the tambourine head (in a very *bravura* manner with dynamic and rhythmic flair) — especially for the first eight bars. **Play the second and third beats of measures 1, 3, 5, and 7 with more importance and deliberation (indicated by *staccato* marks), adding *attitude* to this Spanish dance.** After the downbeat of measure nine to the final *p,* switch to fingertips near the edge of the head.

2. Seventeen Measures before Letter A:
   With the tambourine head facing up, rest the middle of the head on the knee. Brace it with the heels of both hands and play with the fingertips at the edge of the head. **Add a slight *crescendo,* starting on the second measure, for four bars; then, *diminuendo* for three bars.** This also works well for other similar sections.

3. Fifteen Measures before Letter B:
   Coming from the knee position, quickly lift the tambourine with the holding hand at this point and play the first four measures in the center of the head with the fingers. Then, return the tambourine to the knee for the *p* section and play with both hands near the edge for the following four bars. **Repeat this action. With a bit of practice these *piano/forte* transitions can be achieved smoothly.**

4. Three Measures before Letter B (above):
   Do not play these three measures too softly. **Letter B begins a long *diminuendo* to *pp;* so, pacing is important in order to create an even *diminuendo* over these seven measures.**

5. Eleven Measures after Letter B:
   The *poco crescendo,* at eleven measures after Letter B (above), increases up to only one *p.* **Pace this *crescendo* with the strings, horns, and harp.**

6

6. One Measure before Letter C:
    Holding the tambourine, play this section with a braced third finger which helps increase the *crescendo* up to a *forte*. The *crescendo* should be increased only to a strong *mf*. Be sure to start this section at the same *piano* dynamic as the orchestra. Maintain a loose wrist and avoid tension, not to strain the sixteenth notes — allow them to flow.

7. Thirteen Measures before Letter D:
    Using the fist (as in the beginning), play the first four measures into the downbeat of the fifth measure without changing the *ff* dynamic. The remaining ten bars should be played with the fingers in the center of the head. **At this point, the orchestra makes a long *diminuendo* into Letter D. Add this *diminuendo* to the part and as the music gets softer, move towards the rim.** Listen carefully to the orchestra as they may end at Letter D at a *p* or *pp* dynamic. The following is my edited version:

8. Eight Measures after Letter D:
    Remain in the holding position and play this section with the fingers, beginning slightly off the center of the head. During the *diminuendo,* gradually move towards the rim. **Remember, relax the wrist as the dynamic becomes softer.**

9. Letter E to the End:
    Rest the tambourine on the knee and begin to play slightly off the edge of the head, with two fingers, then move to one finger directly on the edge in order to achieve the dying-away (*smorzando*) effect.

No. 7. Habañera

1. <u>Eight Measures before Letter B:</u>
   Carmen sings this aria in the Opera as the orchestra plays this seductive little piece. Play the entire movement while holding the tambourine. **Experiment with how dry to make the tambourine sound by varying how much to muffle the head.** For instance, at the first entrance before Letter B, I like to hear just a little "chick" sound; therefore, I rest the tambourine head on all five fingertips while holding it in a horizontal position, playing off the edge with a braced third finger. **As the phrase ends, it's very appropriate to add a subtle *diminuendo* one beat before Letter B.**

2. <u>Letter C to Letter D:</u>
   Proudly display the tambourine in the holding position and play these eighth notes with a bit of direction towards the downbeat.

3. <u>Four Measures after Letter D to Letter E:</u>
   Listen carefully to the stylized rhythm of the sixteenth notes in the cello to accurately play the part. The tambourine and cello parts are as follows:

4. <u>Final Two Measures:</u>
   Listen carefully to the violins so as to accurately place the final note. The final two measures of the Habañera, including the violin part, are as follows:

No. 11. Danse Bohême

1. <u>Three Measures before Letter D to Letter E:</u>
   I suggest using a tambourine with very sensitive jingles for the opening section to five measures after Letter G. Since the tempo is quick, be careful of the first entrance. **Connect all rolls into the following note and add a slight *tenuto* to the first two syncopated quarter notes.** Begin this section by resting the tambourine face-up on the knee. Play all rolls with a *Braced Third-Finger Roll* and all other notes with the third and fourth fingers of the holding hand. Secure the tambourine on the knee with the heel of the holding hand. The striking hand is now free to execute the rolls.

   Add the dynamic hairpins (notated below) to create a musical flow to the measures. Follow the flute line as you execute this subtle interpretation. At one measure before Letter D, follow the direction of the winds into Letter D. Articulate the notes following the rolls, starting two measures after Letter D, as indicated by the *staccato* marks.

2. <u>Three Measures after Letter E:</u>
   At three measures after Letter E add a slight *diminuendo.*

3. <u>Letter G:</u>
   The orchestration thins out in these four bars into the downbeat of the fifth measure after Letter G; so, I suggest adding a *diminuendo.*

4. <u>Three Measures after Letter I:</u>
   Closely watch the conductor during this *rallentando* since there may be a hold on beat three with an upbeat in the new tempo when the Animato returns:

5. <u>Four Measures after Letter I:</u>
   This Animato tempo (above) is quicker than the opening Animato and keeps pushing forward until the end of the movement. Both the strings and tambourine play at the *mf* level. The melody in the winds is at an *f* level. A steady *crescendo* begins at two measures after Letter K and continues until the *f* at Letter L.

6. <u>Three Measures after Letter L:</u>
From three measures after Letter L to the Più mosso, play these rolls with the
***Open-Hand Thumb Roll* method, connecting them into the third beat.** The *f* on
the "an" of beat three is a *subito f* and sounds more like an *sfz* (*sforzando*) accent —
do not *crescendo* into this note. Execute the end of the roll on the third beat with the
fingers and the "an" of three with the fist. All the rolls begin at the *p* level.

7. <u>Four Measures before Letter M:</u>
The violin part for this section is shown below. To compliment the violin line, I
perform these measures as follows:

Play the single strikes, four measures before Letter M (above), with a braced
third finger, and the rolls at three before Letter M with an *Un-Braced Third*
***Finger Roll.* The note on beat two (following the roll) is played with the thumb**
and the note on the "an" of two is played with the third finger. The final note in
the measure is played with a braced third finger. Repeat this at two measures
before Letter M; then continue with the braced third finger into Letter M.

8. <u>One Measure before Letter N:</u>
Play this section using all fingers somewhat braced with the thumb. **Use an arm**
motion on all *forte* downbeats while playing with a wrist motion to achieve the
soft off-beats. Balance these dynamics slightly under the winds and strings.

9. <u>Six Measures before Letter P:</u>
Watch for an *accelerando* six measures before Letter P into the Presto. At the Presto,
switch from the braced fingers to a fist — but, be sure not to overpower the orchestra!
During the final three measures, hold the instrument high and sustain a
powerful *Standard Shake Roll* popping the final note with a strong accent.

CARNEVAL OVERTURE
Antonin Dvorak

Tambourino

Dvorak's *Carneval Overture* is one of the most frequently requested audition pieces for tambourine in the orchestral repertoire. Since there are so many different techniques, it is a popular gauge of the percussionist's ability on this instrument.

I suggest using a 10 inch tambourine with a double row of copper jingles. The copper jingles produce a solid sound which cuts through the orchestra. Use a brighter-sounding 10 inch tambourine also with a double row of jingles — dryer and more sensitive — for the section between Letters F and L.

Although *Symphonic Repertoire for Percussion Accessories* explores various techniques and ethnic styles of tambourine playing, Dvorak's *Carneval Overture* uses standard orchestral techniques. **Paramount in technical consideration for tambourine playing is the use of the stronger hand when striking the head and the weaker hand for holding the instrument.** Never switch hands in order to accommodate the lack of technical ability.

A particular nemesis for many percussionists is the shake roll. Most players find it easier to execute this technique with the strong hand; however, there is not always time to switch between techniques. **It is crucial to develop the shake roll with the weak hand so the strong hand is always available for articulating rhythms.**

Hold the tambourine in a vertical position, about shoulder height, with the tambourine head facing the player's strong hand. Strike the tambourine with the flat part of the knuckles, in the center of the head, for loud notes and near the edge of the head, with the fingertips, for soft notes.

1. Opening Eight Measures:
   The opening dynamic is one *f*. **Do not be tempted to play too loudly; however, do play with energy and dynamism.** Measure one has an implied accent on the syncopation so as to evoke a festive mood. Measures two and three have a forward-moving direction into measure four. In measures five and six, place the emphasis on the downbeat. Pay special attention to these two measures by "sitting on the pulse" of beats one and three. I explain this to my students as "playing with rhythm and deliberation." In other words, do not rush or push through the tempo. The measure before the repeat bar needs the same forward direction as measures two and three. The following is the actual notation and my edited version:

2. Opening Eight Measures:

The *staccato* indications are played with a very quick short stroke, implying a weak accent. Hold the tambourine fairly flat to get this effect. The "let-ring" signs, in the first measure, and in the first and second endings, imply a longer type of articulation. Accomplish this by holding the tambourine a bit higher while striking "off" the head, allowing the jingles to sustain a bit longer.

Whenever adding articulations and phrasing to music, always play them with subtlety. Playing them as written would be too obvious and overbearing.

3. Measures Four to Six:

The rolls in measures four, five, and six are *Standard Shake Rolls*. **To achieve the emphasis on the downbeat verses the weaker third beat, strike the beginning of the roll with the knuckles and the end of the roll with the fingers.** Then, in measure seven, go back to using the knuckles.

4. Six Measures before Letter A to Five Measures after Letter A:

The measure after the second ending (first measure below) and the measure at Letter A have a *diminuendo* in the score for some of the wind and string instruments. This is also appropriate for the tambourine; so, I have added it below (including the tremolo indication at Letter A — which is missing in the part). **I suggest using a *Standard Shake Roll,* lowering the tambourine while playing to create the *diminuendo*.** Gently landing on beat three with the palm in the middle of the head for both measures will place your hand in the correct position for the next five measures. These measures should be played with the middle finger on the edge of the tambourine head. Place a small accent *(staccato)* on the eighth notes in the third and fourth measures before Letter A, and the third and fourth measures after Letter A. Also, add a *crescendo* up to *mp* two measures before Letter A.

5. Two Measures before Letter B

This roll begins at an *f* dynamic in the part; but, I suggest starting softer at an *mp* level. **It is important not to attack the beginning of the roll.** Use the *Assisted Shake Roll* technique to begin this roll. As you make the *crescendo*, raise the tambourine and continue rolling with the *Standard Shake Roll* into Letter B.

Editor's Note: Dvorak (or the copyist) alternates between using a *tr* (tremolo), two slashes, or three slashes for roll indications. For all practical purposes, there is no difference in this piece.

6. Letter F to M:
   All four of these very soft sections can be executed in two ways:

   a. Rest the palm of the striking hand on the head of the tambourine and tap the rhythms on the edge of the head with the third and fourth fingers.

   b. Dampen the underside of the tambourine with the tips of the holding hand's fingers and with the striking hand; brace the third finger with the thumb while tapping the rhythm on the edge of the head.

   Editor's Note: Some sections, as Letter F below, have *staccato* markings; however, at this soft dynamic, they have no noticeable effect.

7. Five Measures after Letter H:
   Executing a long shake roll can be tiresome on the wrist. **The goal is to create a continuous stream of vibrating jingles that sound like a long tone — without bumps or beats.** Two methods commonly used for achieving a long shake roll is the *Standard Shake Roll* as described in the techniques on page 4, or to hold the tambourine vertically, loosely moving the wrist from front to back. I suggest adding a slight *crescendo* during the final two measures.

8. Two Measure before Letter M:
   Add a *crescendo* at two measures before Letter M into the downbeat of M.

9. Letter Q to One Measure after Letter R:
   Letter Q begins the recapitulation of the original theme. Use the same techniques described in the exposition. The music, beginning at six measures before Letter R, calls for a lighter stroke because of the thinner texture of the orchestration. **I suggest using only two knuckles for the *f* measures and fingertips on the edge of the tambourine for the *p* measures.** For very fast tempos, play the *p* measures by resting the tambourine on the leg and playing with the fingertips of both hands. At Letter R, add an *f* dynamic similar to six measures before Letter R.

10. Eleven after Letter R to the End.
    The section from eleven measures after Letter R to the end employs the *Knee/Fist Method* described on the techniques page.

The question is: "When do I turn the tambourine over so the head faces the knee?" This can be accomplished by quickly pivoting the instrument at the same time the second note of eleven measures after R is played. Or, the tambourine can be pivoted from the roll to the second beat at nine measures before Letter R. The section immediately following this measure will then have to be played with the tambourine upside down.

Once the tambourine is in the knee-fist position, play all strong beats with the fist and weak beats with the knee:

F = Fist
K = Knee

11. Five Measures after Letter T:
    Add a *crescendo* at the fifth measure after Letter T, as indicated below:

14

12. <u>Eight Measures before Letter U:</u>
Stress the eighth notes in this section to bring out the superimposed rhythmic pattern.

13. <u>Letter W:</u>
The tempo is a bit faster at this point (*Poco più mosso)* and the tambourine is the only instrument playing the quarter-note triplets. **If you have fast hands, this can be played with the fist, or you could incorporate the *Knee/Fist Method* with the following pattern:**

14. <u>Eleven Measures before the End:</u>
Again, the tambourine is the only instrument playing this figure; so, maintain a stable rhythm. **I suggest using all fist, or the following knee-fist pattern:**

PETER GRIMES
Benjamin Britten
Storm

Tambourine

The tambourine part in the "Storm" scene from the opera *Peter Grimes* is short but very challenging. The tambourine plays from rehearsal Number 10 to 11. **Use a tambourine that easily responds with one or two rows of very sensitive jingles.** Thumb rolls are necessary throughout the excerpt. I suggest one of the following methods:

    a. **With the tambourine resting on the leg, execute the thumb rolls using a *Braced Third-Finger Roll.*"** Single notes are played with the holding hand.

    b. **Hold the tambourine at shoulder height with the holding hand and play all rolls and single notes using the un-braced third finger.**

I prefer the latter method because the quality of sound and dynamic execution is greater.

    1. <u>Number 10:</u>
    The actual notation for the first measure of the tambourine part is as follows:

Using the above notation, it can be interpreted as follows:

    2. <u>One and Two Measures after Number 10:</u>
    At rehearsal Number 10, Britten has added separate bows and articulations to the bass part; the winds change pitch on the fourth note in both measures.

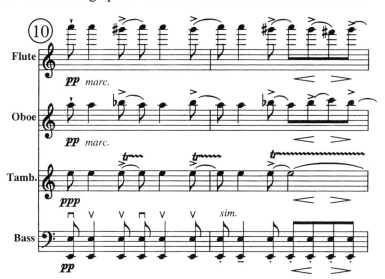

PETER GRIMES by Benjamin Britten
© Copyright 1945 by Boosey & Hawkes Music Publishers Ltd.
Reprinted by permission of Boosey & Hawkes, Inc.

16

If we match the articulation of the other instruments to the tambourine part, the following is a more accurate notation of how this part should be played:

3. <u>Second Measure after Number 10:</u>
All of the long rolls, similar to the one above in the second measure of Number 10, are played as one long roll with only the first accent. There are no other articulations during the roll.

4. <u>Number 10 to Number 11:</u>
The tone of this excerpt should be very dry and without a lot of ring from the head. **To accomplish this, I mute the head with the fingertips of the holding hand and glue a strip of light-grade sandpaper to the area of the head used for thumb rolls.** This produces a drier sound and makes for flawless finger rolls.

5. <u>Entire Excerpt:</u>
The sticking I use for the excerpt is as follows:

     I = Single note with the third finger
     R = Roll with the third finger
     T = Single note with the thumb

6. <u>Entire Excerpt:</u>
The goal of this excerpt is to connect all the rolls smoothly into the single notes. I accomplish this by using the *Un-Braced Third-Finger Roll* method. Since the tempo is on the quick side and in two beats to the measure, execution can be tricky — especially the small hairpin *crescendos.*

Strike the attack of this roll with an arm motion into the head and let the speed and pressure of the hand determine the dynamic. More pressure produces a louder dynamic and lighter pressure, a softer dynamic. With a bit of practice, this technique can be mastered.

7. <u>Entire Excerpt:</u>
   The *ppp* dynamic range prevents the tambourine from standing out. **Think of this dynamic as perfectly blending with the rest of the ensemble.**

8. <u>Sixth, Seventh, and Eighth Measures after Number 10:</u>
   The orchestra makes a *crescendo* from the sixth to the eighth measure after Number 10. **I suggest adding a similar *crescendo* in the tambourine part up to an *mp* or even an *mf*.** The winds and strings (except the bassoon) *crescendo* to an *mf* and *f;* so, the tambourine sound should match them. This has been added to the complete excerpt on page 16.

9. <u>One Measure before Number 11:</u>
   A copy of the first and second oboe parts, at one measure before Number 11, is as follows. **I suggest holding the tambourine a bit more vertical on the final roll and tilting it horizontally for the last note so as to achieve the correct color and articulation.**

PETROUCHKA
Igor Stravinsky
First Part
Tambourine

This brilliant ballet by Stravinsky has two versions that are still performed — the original 1911 Ballet and the 1947 revision. The prominent, more challenging tambourine part is in the latter version. I find that a very bright, metallic, almost noisy tambourine works great for this piece.

1. Number 11 to Four Measures after Number 12 and Number 40 to Number 42: Stravinsky asks for the section after Number 11 to be played by one player using a metal beater. Use a felt mallet on a suspended tambourine (or rest it on a thick towel).

   If two players are available, I recommend splitting the part. **Play these tambourine notes near the edge by bracing the third and fourth fingers with the thumb.** These notes should be played slightly more accented than the triangle and cymbal which creates more interest on the off-beat placement.

2. Three Measures after Number 12 and Three Measures before Number 42: Stravinsky asks for a second player to play the 4-stroke ruff in the above example. An alternative to using a second player is for one player to use a twisting motion for the three grace notes followed by striking the main note.

3. Number 53: Stravinsky often worked closely with his percussionists and was very specific about his intentions. At Number 53, he specifies a thumb roll on beat two, connecting it to an accented third beat. Note that it begins at *forte* with a *crescendo* into a wedge accent in the first measure. The *"sim."* (similar) indication between the first and second measures indicates that this articulation should continue for all of the following measures (see parenthesis in the music example below). **Execute these rolls with the *Open-Hand Thumb Roll* method.**

   The note following the roll can be played with a finger stroke, pivoting from the thumb roll. If more of an accent is needed, use the heel of the hand.

PETROUCHKA by Igor Stravinsky
© Copyright 1912 by Hawkes & Son (London) Ltd.
Revised version: © Copyright 1948 by Hawkes & Son (London) Ltd.
U.S. Copyright Renewed.
Reprinted by permission of Boosey & Hawkes, Inc.

4. <u>Two Measures before Number 56:</u>
   The final roll, two measures before Number 56, should be played as a *Standard Shake Roll*, ending with a fist stroke.

5. <u>One Measure before Number 66 and Three Measures before Number 67:</u>
   Execute these two rolls exactly as Number 53; however, start a bit softer and end the rolls with the heel of the hand.

6. <u>Three Measures after Number 201 to Number 206:</u>
   This tambourine excerpt is often on audition lists. As in most of the other sections, Stravinsky is very specific regarding articulation and types of rolls. The tempo indication is very quick, at 138 to the quarter note, but this excerpt can be performed as fast as 160 to the quarter note. **There is no dynamic indication; however, I suggest beginning at an *mf* and ending at an *f* to match the winds and strings.** Typically, from Number 201 to 205, the dynamic range increases as the orchestra texture thickens.

   All eighth-note rolls in the 2/4 section should have an implied *crescendo*, connect them to the accented note following the rolls. Any of the various tambourine rolls can be used to execute this passage, from the *Open-Hand Thumb Roll*, making a *crescendo* into a finger stroke, or the heel of the hand, to a *Braced Third-Finger Roll* (with the final note played by the holding hand into the knee). Use the technique that achieves the most consistent effect. The following is my edited version of the excerpt:

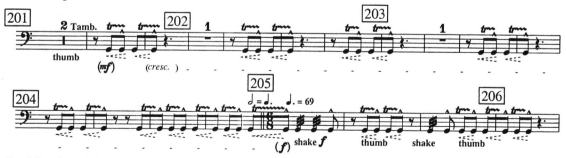

7. <u>Number 205:</u>
   At the 6/8 (Number 205), Stravinsky shows that the indication of a half note equals a dotted quarter note. **This means the pulse of the previous half note in 2/4 time now equals the dotted quarter note in 6/8 time.** Note that the long rolls in the first and third measures, after Number 205, are played as *Standard Shake Rolls* with the holding hand. Be careful at Number 206 because the strings are in 2/4 time at this point and have a run, leading into the second half of the bar.

Polovetsian Dances

Alexander Borodin

Tamburino

Alexander Borodin's *Polovetsian Dances*, from the opera Prince Igor, are commonly played as a suite without chorus. Dances Number 8 and 17 are usually played together as an orchestral suite.

No. 8 - Dance of the Polovetsian Maidens

1. Opening:
   This piece is in 6/8 and usually conducted in one beat to the bar throughout the entire movement. There has always been some confusion as to the small circular symbol that appears throughout both pieces:

There are many different interpretations to this symbol, but, as my editor pointed out a translation from a Russian percussion book refers to this symbol as a type of "slap" stroke. **Musically, it should sound like a bright accented note.** There are several ways to achieve this, all with very different results. I suggest trying all the different styles and choosing one that is best for you.

The first is a classical orchestral approach in which the tambourine is basically held with the weak hand and played with the strong hand. An alternative is to rest the tambourine on the knee and play with both hands. In either position, all the notes with a circle above them are played more towards the center of the head (either with the fingers or the knuckles).

In the quicker passages, which are usually conducted in one to a bar, such as the opening of No. 8 (above), play the tambourine on the knee (as mentioned) with two hands. **Strike the downbeats slightly toward the center of the head and all the other notes towards the rim.** At letter A, you will have arrived at this passage with the tambourine on your knee, which can then be picked up with the holding hand while playing the quarter notes with the other hand.

2. Nine Measures after Letter A:
   At nine after A the following rhythm is written:

Since the circles are on beats 1 & 2, I found a great way to get the thicker accented color of these beats while getting crisper unaccented upbeats. **Hold the tambourine fairly flat with the holding hand with the head facing up. With the playing hand, keep the third and fourth fingers together and angle these two fingers with the thumb in the shape of a U. Using this hand position, play beats 1 & 2 with the thumb towards the center of the head, and play the upbeats with the third and**

fourth fingers on the edge of the tambourine. Pivoting the wrist back and forth will allow you to play this rhythm in many different speeds and dynamics. Strike the tambourine with a small motion in the beginning of the passage and increase the motion in the *crescendo*, which starts eight measures before Letter B.

Another way to play this is to add another player. One player will play just the notes with a circle over them while the other player plays the un-circled notes — basically ignoring the accented circled notes. This can be very effective because each player can have a different instrument, highlight the differing colors needed for the circled notes versus the un-circled ones.

The last way to play this is with a much more ethnic tradition and is basically the same technique explained in the *Roman Carnival Overture* — the Southern Italian style. The tambourine is held in an upright position by the holding hand with the head facing away from the player. **The circled notes or "slaps" are struck both with the thumb and the base of the thumb by pivoting the wrist into the middle of the head.** Refer to page 26 in the *Roman Carnival Overture* to review the strokes. Instructions for playing the opening and nine measures after Letter A are as follows:

a = Thumb and base of thumb near the center of the head with an accent stroke
b = Back of index finger near the top of the head
c = Third, fourth, and fifth finger near the bottom of the head
d = Thumb and base of thumb near the center of the head without an accent stroke

Because of the triplet pattern in the beginning, try to give extra force to the downbeats of each measure and not on beat two. This style of playing can be executed at many dynamic ranges and with extremely fast tempos once mastered.

3. <u>Four Measures before Letter B:</u>
   The downbeat at four measures before Letter B can be played with the heel of the hand to get a strong *sfz* followed by a shake roll. Since there is a descending chromatic scale in the clarinets into a *p* dynamic, a more accurate representation would be:

The roll (above) can be struck with an aggressive slap stroke, immediately going into a roll with an *Assisted Shake Roll.*

4. <u>Ten Measures after Letter C to End of Movement:</u>
   The rest of this movement consists of the 5/8 patterns plus material previously discussed at the beginning of the movement.

5. Nine Measures after Letter C:

    If using a classical orchestral approach, the material at ten measures after Letter C in the *p* dynamic can be played with the tambourine on the knee. Like the beginning, play the down beats more toward the center of the head and use the following sticking to make the 5/8 pattern smooth.

    The dynamics of all the 5/8 patterns should slightly balance under the Oboe and Clarinets. These instruments are always written at a louder dynamic but one should approach it with a balanced concept. For instance, at ten measures after Letter F, the tambourine is marked at *pp* and the winds are at *mf.* The tambourine player should listen carefully and play at a level that supports the winds.

6. Three Measures before Letter D:

    At three measures before D, the tambourine can be played with a combination *Knee/Fist Method.* Play the downbeats with the fist; then, switch to fingers and fist for all other notes. From three measures before Letter D, it would look like this:

7. Nine Measures after Letter C:

    If using the Southern Italian style, all dynamics can be played in the up position with the following sticking:

    Fingering:

    a = Thumb near the center of the head
    b = Third, fourth, and fifth fingers on the edge of the head
    c = Thumb near the edge of the head

8. <u>Nine Measures after Letter D</u>:
   At nine measures after Letter D, the dotted-quarter note, in the second beat of the first measure, should be a quarter note like the rest of the notes in this pattern. **The majority of the orchestra has an accent on the second beat of the third, fifth, and seventh bar; this accent should also be played by the tambourine player as well.**

9. <u>Four Measures before Letter E</u>:
   The roll at four measures before Letter E should be the same as four measures before Letter B but with a bit more volume because of the thicker orchestration.

10. <u>Final Ten Measures</u>:
    The last 10 bars of the piece should read as the following:

Note that the original part does not have slap marks on the downbeats of the 5/8 bars; however, I have added them along with some additional dynamics in the measures of rolls.

No. 17 - Polovetsian Dance with Chorus

The same type of symbol (small circles) exists in this movement and the same choices of orchestral versus ethnic tambourine playing can be chosen.

1. <u>Letter C:</u>
Letter C is in a brisk 4/4 time and the small circles reappear over the "an" of beat 2 and 4; but, this is incorrect. **The slap stroke should be on the "an" of beats 1 and 3, which matches the articulation in the bassoons and horns.**

Since virtually the whole orchestra is at an *f* dynamic at letter C, the tambourine player should balance this with an *mf* (as indicated).

2. <u>Eight Measures before Letter D:</u>
The figure, eight measures before Letter D, and eight measures after Letter V, should be played with an *Open Hand Thumb Roll*, connecting into the "an" of beat one by using the heel of the hand. This helps to color the accent in the accompaniment figure. The two remaining notes on beats 2 and 4 can be played with the second, third, and fourth fingers.

3. <u>Eight Measures after Letter D:</u>
The *Assisted Shake Roll* should be used eight measures after Letter D. Hold the tambourine very low when starting this roll and raise the instrument during the *crescendo* (removing the assisting hand) to end the roll with a nice pop on the last *sf* note.

4. Letter N and Letter U:
   The sections at Letters N and U are marked Presto and are usually conducted in one beat to the bar — so be ready for the quick tempo. **All the rolls at letter N should employ the *Open Hand Thumb Roll.*** The end of the rolls should be played by pivoting the hand so the fingers strike the edge of the tambourine. Some parts have this section marked as *p*, but it clearly should be an *f* to match the horns. Also, the beginning of the rolls should have an emphasis, ending a bit less on beat 2.

The repeat of this section at letter U is missing the *diminuendo* at eight measures before V. **However, the descending melodic line of the French horns suggests adding a slight *diminuendo.***

5. Final 5 Measures:
   In the last 5 measures, add a slight *crescendo*, leading with a nice pop on the final note to end the movement.

A ROMAN CARNIVAL
Hector Berlioz

Overture

2 Tamburini

Roman Carnival Overture by Hector Berlioz evokes scenes of festivities and dancing. The inspiration for *Roman Carnival* occurred when Berlioz travelled to Rome during carnival season. **I am assuming that many of the faster rhythmic patterns in the Allegro vivace section were taken from Southern Italian tambourine players during the carnival. Therefore, I feel compelled to talk about this particular style of playing.**
The holding position of the tambourine is vertical as opposed to the normal angled position. Hold it directly in front of the chest with the head facing away from the body. The thumb is placed on the inside of the frame and the fingers on the outside of the head.
Since the tambourine is not in the angled position, the jingles have a more open sound which is appropriate for this music.
The striking hand is utilized as follows:

  a. The inside of the thumb strikes the center of the head
  b. The inside (flat) part of the third, fourth, and fifth fingertips strike half way between the center and the edge of the head
  c. With the palm facing outward, strike the top of the head with the back of the forefinger
  d. With the palm of the hand facing the head, rotate between the thumb, striking the center of the head, and the lower three fingers (not the forefinger) striking near the edge

This method of playing may seem awkward at first, but it is actually easier to execute the rhythms and has a fluidity which cannot be attained through conventional methods. Once this technique is practiced and mastered, these rhythmic figures can be played at extremely fast tempi.
The score and parts call for two tambourine players who double the entire part.
This overture can be played with a combination of orchestral and Southern Italian techniques, providing a variety of colors to the music.

1. Number 3:
    For this section, hold the tambourine in the standard horizontal position, and strike the rim with the braced third finger. This figure is light and bouncy over the lyrical melody in the strings. **The striking hand should not rest on the head, allowing the tambourine jingles to ring.** The 32nd and 16th notes on the third beats need a full, rich sound. So, play the third beat of the measures closer to the center of the head, gradually moving towards the edge during the 16th notes while making a *diminuendo* into the next measure.

2. Number 5:

These rolls are best played as thumb rolls. I connect the first two rolls into the following eighth notes since there is a *diminuendo* into the third beats at the *p* level. **Use the *Un-Braced Third-Finger Roll* for the first two measures and the *Open-Hand Thumb Roll* for the third measure.** Also, be aware, directly at Number 5, there is a *poco animato*; therefore, the tempo will be quicker than the previous measures.

3. Twenty Measures after Number 6:

Begin the Allegro vivace section using the braced third finger while holding the tambourine in the Southern Italian vertical position — angling the tambourine so the jingles are at rest. Remain in this position, using the fist at Number 7. Then, return to the vertical position after Number 8 so as to be ready for the Southern Italian techniques through Number 10:

4. Nine Measures after Number 8:

Move the tambourine into the vertical position and play this section using the Southern Italian technique as indicated below:

This entire Allegro vivace section is in a fast, two beats to the measure; however, many conductors conduct it in one beat to the measure — so count carefully!

5. Number 14:

A rhythm modulation occurs at Number 14 where the previous dotted half note (in the 6/8 section) now becomes a half note in these 2/4 measures. **Therefore, the beat is the same, but the eighth notes in the 2/4 measures are slower.** Use the *Knee-Fist Method* for the sixteenth notes.

6. <u>One Measure before Number 17:</u>
The final note in this measure should not only be short, but also bright and accented. Strike it with the fist in the center of the head to get a nice "pop."

Editor's Note: Berlioz indicates the term "short" in three languages: German, Italian, and English. A staccato/wedge accent is very appropriate here.

7. <u>Ten Measures before Number 19:</u>
This section occurs in a lighter orchestration with the strings; so, do not play too loudly. The following "sticking" works well using the Southern Italian technique:

8. <u>Six Measures after Number 19:</u>
Begin the roll at the sixth measure after Number 19 with the *Assisted Shake Roll* technique, raising the tambourine up as you *crescendo* into the 2/4 measure.

Play the eighth notes after Number 19 very deliberate and strong. Notice the eighth notes begin with an *sf* indication on the first note.

9. <u>Number 20:</u>
Add a slight *crescendo* into beat two on the first and third measures after Number 20.

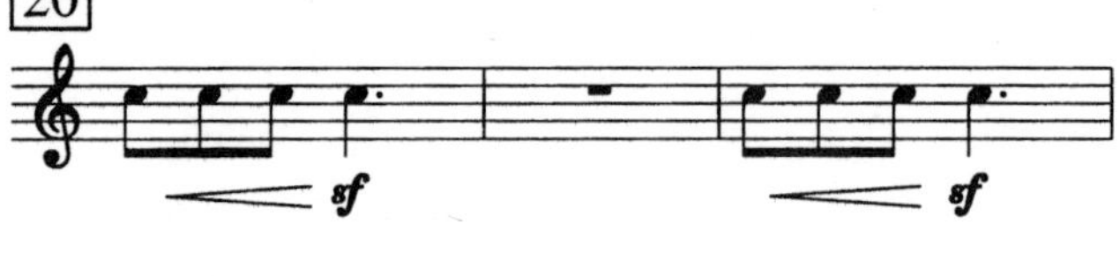

10. <u>Final Three Measures:</u>
Use a *Standard Shake Roll* three measures from the end and add a *crescendo* into the final note of the Overture.

SCHEHERAZADE
N. Rimsky Korsakow

Suite Symphonique

Tamburino

I. II. Tacet
III.

I use two tambourines for this work: a very delicate one for soft dynamics and a general, all-around tambourine with bronze jingles for everything else — both instruments should have double rows of jingles.

1. Letter E
   The tambourine dynamic should perfectly match with the triangle. Rest the palm of the striking hand on the head of the tambourine while striking the notes with the third finger near the edge of the head.

2. Five Measures after Letter F:
   Play this and all similar sections with a braced third finger. **I perform the roll in the eighth and sixteenth measures after Letter F with an *Un-Braced Third Finger Roll*.** Add a slight *diminuendo* into the final note, striking it with the thumb.

3. Letter G:
   The written dynamic at Letter G is *pp*. I find this to be too soft. **I recommend playing this section at *mp*.** Balance this dynamic with the entire percussion section.

4. Three Measures before Letter I:
   Since the orchestration is still thin, I suggest continuing with the delicate tambourine at three measures before Letter I. The measure before each of these two entrances broadens a bit (slight *rit.*); so, carefully watch the conductor. **I recommend playing the two grace notes with a *twisting motion* of the wrist while striking the main note with the knuckles.**

5. Nine Measures after Letter P (Final Four Measures):
    Using an *Un-Braced Third-Finger Roll*, connect each roll to its release note. Add a subtle *diminuendo* (as a nice touch) to these measures. Notice the addition of the slurs which indicates a smooth connection to the note.

IV.

See page 45, in the triangle excerpt of this movement, for a lengthy discussion of performance issues concerning the 2/8 vs. 3/8 time signatures.

1. Thirteen Measures after the "Allegro molto e frenetico:"
    Perform this extended roll using the *Assisted-Shake Roll*. Hold the tambourine low (at the knee) for the *pp* and lift it up as you make a *crescendo* into a *forte*. Strike the final note with the fist.

2. Twenty Four Measures before Letter A (Vivo):
    The Vivo will probably be conducted in one beat to the measure. **Listen to the viola part (below) in order to place the rhythms accurately.**

3. Letter B:
    These four measures, repeated four times, are all phrased to the downbeat in the fourth measure. **Add a slight accent to this downbeat to articulate the passage with the orchestra.** I suggest playing this part with the fist at the indicated *mf* dynamic.

4. <u>Letter F:</u>
The tambourine part is written to imply two beats to the measure. It should actually be played with one beat to the measure, in a 3/8 feel, to accommodate the flute melody. The following examples show how this rhythm is written and how it should be played. The interaction between the flute and tambourine part at four measures after Letter F is as follows:

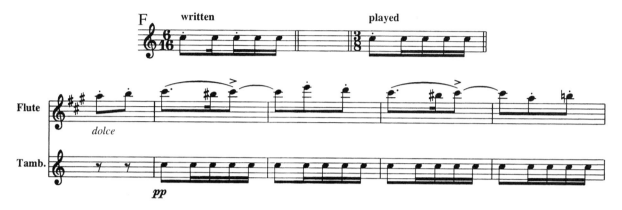

Rest the center of the tambourine on the knee with the head facing up. Brace the tambourine with the forearms and heel of the hands, striking the head with the fingers. **Begin this section a couple of inches away from the edge; then, move closer to the rim to help with the *diminuendo*.**

5. <u>Four Measures before Letter L:</u>
This section is unique and a lot of fun to play. The entire orchestra is in a 6/16 pulse; the tambourine follows the cymbal part, playing the same rhythms. Hold the tambourine in the "head-down" position for this section. **I suggest flipping the tambourine from the "head-up" position to the "head-down" position after playing the eighth note at four measures before Letter L.**

Keep the tambourine in the "flipped" position for the remainder of the movement.

6. <u>Four Measures before Letter O</u>:
   Rest the tambourine on the knee and play on the rim (head down) with the third and fourth fingers of each hand. **Even though the dynamic is *pp*, dig in and play with a *quasi-marcato* touch.** Also, take note that nine measures after Letter O, the winds have a hairpin *crescendo* and *diminuendo*. Do not be influenced by this — play *sempre pp* throughout.

   The tambourine complements the flute and oboe at this point. Carefully listen to these instruments since the timpani and violas are playing four sixteenth notes to the measure (2/8) against the 6/16 triplet feel in the winds and tambourine.

7. <u>Fifteen Measures after Letter W</u>:
   Use the *Knee-Fist Method* as indicated below. Alternating the fist and knee strokes works well for this excerpt.

8. <u>Thirteen Measures before Letter X (Allegro non troppo e maestoso)</u>:
   A slight broadening may occur before the Allegro; so, watch the conductor!

SYMPHONY No. 4
Johannes Brahms

I. II. u IV. Tacet
TRIANGEL

III.

In all of Brahms four symphonies, he only used one percussion instrument (the triangle) for one movement in the Third Movement of the Fourth Symphony. **There are a few subtleties that need to be addressed for this work: differing colors, roll endings, and articulation.**

Use a large triangle that measures eight to nine inches. **The range of overtones is important when choosing a triangle.** Be sure it contains both low and high qualities when struck. **It is also nice to have a triangle that produces different colors, depending on where it is struck.** I use a medium-heavy beater made of bronze. Do not be tempted to use a small, thin beater for the soft sections. **A small beater will sacrifice tone quality.** Use a light stroke with a medium-heavy beater and play with the tip to produce a soft sound.

1. Five Measures before Letter B:
   Notice that the tremolo indication above the note goes beyond the first beat of the next measure. **Roll through the "an" of beat one, leaving a slight space before the rest on beat two.**

   All of the sixteenth-note figures should be played on the "dry" side without overplaying. Do not destroy the overtones by playing too loudly. This can be achieved by slightly dampening the very top of the triangle with the little finger of the holding hand. **Perform the sixteenth-note figures with an emphasis on the first beat and muffle the rests two measures before Letter B.**

2. Letter C:
   For this delicate section of the piece, find an area on the triangle that has many high overtones. **The _staccato_ markings can be achieved by slightly dampening each note with the fourth finger of the holding hand.**

3. Seven Measures after Letter D:
   This section is a matter of much debate. The question is: Are the half notes marked with two slashes, played as rolls or articulated as sixteenth notes? Actually, they are both! **Think of the section as a slow, measured roll.** Brahms also distinguishes a roll indication with the "tr" sign; so, these notes should definitely be played as articulated sixteenth notes.

34

With a bit of practice, very even sixteenth notes can be played using two legs of the triangle. I get the best results by loosely holding the beater and playing the rhythms with a very limber wrist action.

Another way to perform this section is by suspending the triangle and playing it with two beaters; however, the triangle's tone is not as pure and the character of the sixteenth notes may sound too mechanical.

Beginning at the *f* on the fourteenth measure after Letter D, muffle the sound during the following rests. At the eighteenth measure after Letter D, increase the dynamic so it is louder than the previous *f*.

4. <u>Letter F:</u>
   Allow this note to sustain and play it with as much beauty as possible.

5. <u>Nine Measures after Letter I:</u>
   Perform the roll, nine measures after Letter I, with extra force (*più f*) to balance the strong F dominant chord in the orchestra.

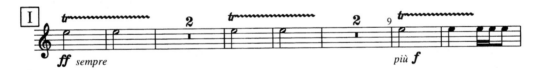

6. <u>Seven Measures before Letter K:</u>
   The *staccato* indications on the quarter notes of the original part in these measures should be played as accents.

7. <u>Letter K:</u>
   Articulate the note following the rolls at Letter K.

CAPRICCIO ESPAGNOL
N. A. Rimsky Korsakow

I. & III. Alborado.

Triangolo

The triangle part in this symphonic suite demands a variety of techniques. The use of one-handed rhythmical playing between the two legs of the instrument is preeminent. In order to play the rhythms evenly, and with the correct pulse and nuances, is important to master this technique.

1. Opening to Letter C:
    The opening of both *Alborado* movements is festive and requires a large triangle (11 or 12 inches). The triangle part begins with two slashes over the notes, indicating abbreviated sixteenth notes — not three slashes — which indicates a roll. Slightly muffle the triangle with a finger of the holding hand, allowing the rhythm to be heard. **Do not overplay!**

2. Fourteen Measures after Letter C to the End:
    Some scores notate this part as sixteenth notes; however, I believe this section should be played as rolls. The dynamic is very soft (*ppp*) and this delicate roll poses technical challenges. Use a brighter-sounding triangle with a more shimmering quality than in the opening section, and strike it with a medium to small beater. If the beater is perpendicular to the instrument, it will strike the "nodal" area of the triangle and produce a sound with fewer overtones. Therefore, I recommend lowering the striking hand, and playing at a 45 degree angle to produce more overtones.

IV. Scena e Canto gitano.

1. <u>Fifteen Measures after Letter L thru Harp Cadenza</u>
   I suggest using a small, bright triangle for the first three delicate notes and the extended roll during the harp cadenza.

   Editor's Note: The composer uses a *tr* indication for the roll during the harp cadenza instead of three slashes. This is frequently seen in percussion notation and, for all purposes, both indications refer to the same roll. Also, notice the *smorz.* directive (*dying away*). The "*dying-away*" effect should be added during the final measure of the roll.

   Listen to the oboe cue at four measures before the triangle entrance to the cadenza. **Maintain the roll at the *pp* dynamic throughout the cadenza.**

2. <u>Letter P:</u>
   Letter P is conducted in two beats to the measure. These triplets are rather quick and flamboyant. Increase the dynamic from *p* to *mp* at Letter P. Letter Q should be played at *mf*.

3. <u>Seven Measures before the End of the Movement:</u>
   There is a slight *animato* at this point into Movement V. This is not indicated in the part.

V. Fandango asturiano

The *Fandango* begins with an *attacca* from the previous movement; so be ready!

The fourth movement pulse of a dotted quarter note ♩. becomes the dotted half note ♩. in the fifth movement.

1. First Four Measures:
    This movement is conducted in one beat to the measure; therefore, the speed of the sixteenth notes is very fast. It is feasible to play all of this movement with one hand; however, do not compromise the rhythm. If it is a struggle to articulate the rhythms with one hand, suspend the triangle and play with two beaters. Place an emphasis on the downbeat of each measure.

V. Fandango asturiano

2. Five Measures after Letter T:
    This section is fairly exposed; so, execute the rhythms accurately and play with confidence — keeping a very steady tempo.

3. Two Measures before Letter U:
    The two measures before Letter U are notated as abbreviated sixteenth notes in the part; however, they should be articulated as a continuous roll (shown below). **The final note should be played very short and with an accent.**

4. Letter V:
    The score and parts do not indicate a dynamic at Letter V. I suggest playing this section at an *mf* level. The tempo may be too fast to play on one leg of the triangle. Experiment with one beater or using two beaters on two legs of the suspended triangle. The tempo may broaden at one measure before Letter W.

5. Letter W:
    Play these measures as rolls and with an emphasis on the downbeats.

6. <u>Letter X</u>:
There is a feeling the music wants to continuously move forward at Letter X. **Watch the conductor as the tempo may increase into the Coda.**

7. <u>Nine Measures after Letter X (Coda)</u>:
The Coda is conducted in a rapid, two beats to the measure. **While the dynamic is marked as *ff*, play with a bouncy style, but not too heavy or overbearing.**

8. <u>Four Measures before Letter Y</u>:
At four measures before Letter Y, be aware the rest of the percussion players are *tacet* for two measures; so, play with confidence. Rimsky-Korsakov (or his copyist) continually alternated between the use of two and three slashes for the different percussion parts. **I suggest playing them all as sixteenth notes.**

9. <u>Letter Y</u>:
Play the final quarter note of these measures short and with an accent.

10. <u>Letter Z</u>:
Play measures 1, 3, 5, 8, and 10 after Letter Z with a bit of forward direction into the end of the measure. Carefully watch the conductor since the measures before the Presto may move ahead.

11. <u>Final Six Measures</u>:
As before, play these roll indications as sixteenth notes. **The quarter notes, two and three measures from the end, should be played as eighth notes (muffled). The final note should sustain.** My interpretation is as follows:

PIANO CONCERTO No. 1
Franz Liszt

The *Liszt Piano Concerto No. 1* is one of the few pieces that features the triangle as a solo instrument. In fact, the triangle begins the third movement, by itself, with a simple four-note motive. **Liszt added a remark, saying the triangle should be played "in a rhythmical manner with resonant precision."** Sometimes the triangle player sits at the front of the orchestra, right next to the piano, because of its prominent role.

I use a seven-inch brass triangle to highlight its brilliance, yet still possessing a shimmering tone quality. A medium or medium-light beater, made of steel, works best.

It is worth noting that the four movements of this concerto are continuous; that is, without breaks. The second movement ends with a piano trill under a low clarinet melody. The third movement begins on the last note of the clarinet melody.

1. Allegretto vivace after Letter E:
   Carefully count from the beginning of the movement and adhere to the strict rhythmic clarity. **Be sure the sixteenth notes are played on the "quick" side to avoid confusing them with a triplet rhythm.** Playing the sixteenth notes in this "crisp" manner will add to the brilliance of the rhythm. This is accomplished by adding an extra *snap* of the wrist to the notes. It also helps to slightly mute the top of the triangle with a finger of the holding hand which helps with articulation. **Although the eighth notes are marked with a *staccato* indication, do not choke them.** Allow the final eighth note to ring for its full value. Although the dynamic is marked as *pp*, it is a solo and must be balanced with the solo piano melody.

2. Four Measures before Letter F:
   Carefully listen to the piano in order to place the two notes accurately. **Raise the dynamic level to *p* to match the solo line.** Editor's Note: Notice, the first eighth-note rest, at four measures before Letter F, is missing the dot in the original part.

40

3. <u>Seven Measures after Letter F:</u>
Allow all of the single notes to sustain. These notes are solos. I also suggest adding a "vibrato" to the sound by shaking the holding hand after striking each note.

4. <u>Six Measures before Letter G:</u>
The opening solo recurs at six measures before Letter G; however, the dynamic is now a *piano (p)* instead of a *pianissimo (pp).*

5. <u>Allegro marziale animato before Letter K:</u>
At this point, I suggest using a larger steel triangle with less shimmering overtones so as to match the heavier orchestration.

Notice that Liszt indicates a quarter note with two slashes — the abbreviation for sixteenth notes. The written-out notation for these measures is as follows:

I perform these measures with one beater, using the lower and side leg of the triangle. Keep the beater parallel to the ground and evenly execute the rhythms. **Since the woodwinds play off the triangle part, all sixteenth notes must be uniform.**

Notice, in the above music example, the *crescendo* actually begins on the third beat of the measure and continues until the final note in the following measure. This happens again at five measures before Letter K.

6. <u>Eleven and Fifteen Measures after Letter L:</u>
Just a reminder: At these two entrances after Letter L, the dynamic is *p* with no crescendo.

7. Sixteen Measures before Letter M:
    The solo motive returns at sixteen measures after Letter M. Be sure to line up with
    the sixteenth notes in the piano. **These notes move quite fast; so, trust the
    conductor and play precisely with the beat.**

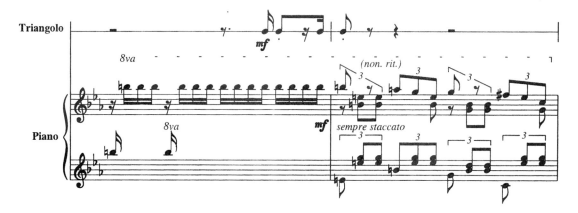

8. Letter M;
    For this section, I use a smaller, brighter triangle with many overtones. The
    "Più mosso" immediately causes a tempo increase at letter M.

9. Four Measures before Letter N:
    **The sixteenth rhythms, four measures before Letter N, can be played louder
    than the written *p* indication in order to balance with the *f* in the winds.** Also,
    add a *crescendo* at two measures before Letter N.

Editor's Note: Liszt also omits the *staccato* indications here. For all practical
purposes, they may be added as shown above.

SCHEHERAZADE
N. Rimsky-Korsakow

Triangolo

The triangle is used in the second, third, and fourth movements of *Scheherazade*. A six or seven inch triangle, struck with brass beaters, works well for the second and third movements. A slightly larger triangle, with a few exceptions, works well for the fourth movement.

II.

1. Entire Second Movement:
   This movement is fairly straightforward. Although there are many *rubati* measures, in all cases, the triangle is not involved.

2. Eighteen Measures after Letter G to Letter H:
   This section is conducted in one beat to the measure. Allow the triangle to ring throughout the movement without any muffling. **However, the final entrance before Letter H should be muffled by beat three.**

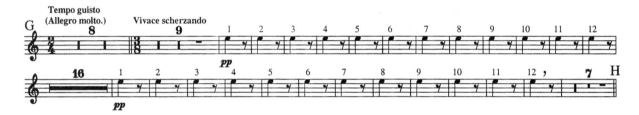

3. Nine Measures after Letter I to Letter K:
   Unlike the *pp* indication after Letter G, the entrance after Letter I is only one *p*. Therefore, play this with more fullness of sound, letting the triangle sustain. Muffle the final note before Letter K on the downbeat of the following measure.

   Listen to the light and bouncy dotted-triplet figure in the winds, starting at the triangle entrance after Letter I, in order to place the triangle note properly on the second beat of the measures.

4. Nine Measures after Letter K:
   The triangle entrance after Letter K now plays part of the triplet rhythm with the winds. **Try to perfectly blend with the winds in this section and let the figure lead into the downbeat of the next measure.**

Birth of Kije

Van Impe

- Practice Consistent Ruffs
    - more closed

- Make Sure flams are not to wide

- Softer

Scheherazade

- consistent dynamics -beg.

- Practice Slow with closed Ruffs

5. Five Measures after Letter P:
These rolls are difficult because they encompass a wide dynamic range and require a connection into a *sfz* downbeat. The dynamic goes from *p* to *ff* in a very short period of time. **Start at the very tip of the beater in one of the corners of the triangle; then, move to the middle of the beater as the *crescendo* builds.** Increase the *crescendo* near the end of each measure. Don't let the last note after each roll sustain for more than the written eighth note. However, the single note, after the three measures of rolls, should ring a bit longer. Allow it to fade out by muffling the sound with a finger of the holding hand.

6. Final Measure:
The final note of this movement is very short!

III.

1. Letter E:
The tambourine and triangle are the only two instruments with a *ppp* dynamic at Letter E. Most other instruments have a *pp*, but the flute and clarinet have an *f*. **Balance the triangle dynamic with the tambourine. Both players should listen to the solo flute line (doubled by the clarinet) for accuracy.** Play the three eighth notes in the triangle as part of a long phase with the flute. The following is the interaction between the flute (doubled by the clarinet), triangle, and tambourine:

2. Five Measures after Letter F to Four Measures before Letter I:
Allow all the quarter notes between Letter F and Letter I to sustain for a full dotted-quarter note value and muffle on the downbeat.

44

3. Letter G:
    The orchestration is thicker at Letter G with the entrance of the brass instruments; therefore, at this point raise the dynamic level.

4. Four Measures before Letter I:
    The second and fourth measures before Letter I are usually performed with a slight *allargando*. **Listen carefully to the trumpet part to accurately place the downbeats after the rolls.** Begin the rolls without any discernable attack by starting them at the very tip of the beater.

5. Final Four Measures:
    Lightly muffle the triangle with a finger of the holding hand for these measures. **Listen carefully to the two pick-up notes in the flute (which occur during a *molto rit*).** Keep a strict tempo from the downbeat and add a slight *diminuendo* until the end.

IV.

1. Allegro molto e frenetico:
    Movement IV presents many technical challenges. Use a nine-inch triangle for the opening with a medium-sized steel beater.

    This Allegro molto begins with a robust *f* dynamic (after the violin cadenza) with a very quick tempo (usually in two beats to the measure). This first entrance is properly marked with three slashes, indicating a roll. The following rolls from the thirteenth measure are marked with only two slashes. One exception is the three slashes on the seventeenth measure; however, the score has only two slashes, indicating abbreviated sixteenth notes. **Regardless, play all these measures as rolls.** The indicated *crescendo* goes to an *f* level on the final note. I suggest adding an accent here. The following is the edited version of this excerpt:

2. <u>Vivo before Letter A:</u>
The score indicates the metronome marking as quarter or dotted quarter equals 88. This is not indicated in the part. **The 2/8, 6/16 or 3/8 time signatures indicate the measures can have two or three eighth notes per measure.** The 6/16 and 3/8 each indicate a three eighth note value — the only difference is how they are phrased. In 6/16, the notes are phrased in two groups of three. In 3/8, the notes are phrased in three groups of two. The following is an example of the notation:

Since the score indicates that both the quarter and dotted quarter notes are played at mm = 88, the effect is that the group of three sixteenths in the 6/16 measure will sound as triplets against groups of two sixteenth notes in a 2/8 measure. **The entire Vivo section is conducted in one beat to the measure.**

3. <u>Letter A:</u>
Allow all notes to sustain at Letter A:

4. <u>Letter D:</u>
Letter D is an interesting section with regard to tempi. Letter D begins with a bassoon solo for three bars:

5. <u>Four Measures after Letter D:</u>
The fourth through seventh bars after Letter D are marked *"Un poco pesante"* in the score; but, it is not indicated in the part. **These measures are conducted in a slower tempo with three beats to the bar.**

6. <u>Nine Measures before Letter E:</u>
The ninth measure before Letter E immediately goes back to the fast two beats to the measure where the triangle plays on the second half of the measure. The *pesante* returns again at five measures before Letter E and the rapid two beats to the measure continue from Letter E. **Be ready for these sudden shifts in tempo — they are not gradual changes.** The following is the flute and triangle part for nine measures before Letter E:

7. <u>Four Measures before Letter F:</u>
This single note should be short and slightly accented.

8. <u>Letter K to Letter M:</u>
The quarter notes at Letter K are notated with three slashes (indicating a roll); however, I suggest playing them as thirty-second notes (which would be at roll speed). It helps to line up the sixteenth-note rhythms in the viola and cello sections. Be aware that some of the orchestra plays in 2/8 and other sections in 3/8 (6/16). I suggest listening to the woodwinds who play in two beats to the measure. The following illustrates how these three groups of instruments look in the score:

Whether using a roll or thirty-second notes, it is appropriate to play the triangle with one hand (using the lower and upper legs) with a strict thirty-second note rhythm.

9. <u>Letter O:</u>
Match the dynamic texture at this point. I suggest adding a *tenuto* mark on all quarter note downbeats.

10. <u>Twenty One Measures after Letter P to Letter Q:</u>
This section is doubled by the tambourine and played in unison with the flute, oboe, bassoon, and French horn. **Because of the light orchestration, do not play too loudly; however, it must have spirit and energy!** I suggest playing all three notes on the bottom leg of the triangle, slightly muting it with a finger of the holding hand.

The wind players have an accent on the eighth note of each figure and an *sf* on the final note at Letter Q; so, I have added them to the music below:

11. <u>Seventeen Measures after Letter V:</u>
Articulate the rolls as thirty-second notes after Letter V with the piccolo. **Play with intensity, but not too soft.**

12. <u>Four Measures before Letter W:</u>
The four notes before Letter W are played short and with an accent.

13. <u>Letter W to Allegro non troppo e maestoso:</u>
The tempo increases at the Spiritoso. Articulate these rhythms with a slight *staccato* feel. It is possible to play everything in this section with one beater; although, for more control, two beaters can be used with a suspended triangle. **Never compromise the rhythm!**

14. <u>Fifteen Measures before the Allegro non troppo e maestoso:</u>
These abbreviated notes are played as articulated thirty-second notes. Add an implied *crescendo* into each downbeat and exaggerate the following eighth notes (including the three measures before the first measure of the thirty-second notes) by adding an accent. Usually, conductors add a *ritard* into the downbeat of the 6/4 Allegro section.

15. <u>Allegro non troppo e maestoso:</u>
This section is the return of the first-movement theme. **Execute all the sixteenth notes in a *legato* manner, letting the instrument ring.** The rolls after Letter X should *crescendo* into the downbeats. I suggest adding the downbeat into the seventh measure after Letter X.

The Rite of Spring
Igor Stravinsky

Part One

Bass Drum

Rite of Spring, Stravinsky's ballet in two parts, is one of the most revolutionary compositions of the Twentieth Century. The bass drum serves as a catalyst for color and aggression. **I use two bass drums for this work, a standard 36 x 20 inch drum on a hoop stand and a single- headed 40 inch drum tuned to Bb.** I use the 36 inch drum throughout the piece unless otherwise mentioned. The 40 inch drum looks as if it was sawed down the center of the shell and is very effective for this composition. I use standard bass drum mallets with varying head shapes and hardness. I will be more specific as we proceed.

1. One Measure before Number 22:
   In order to place this entrance accurately, listen to the triplet figure played by the timpani on the first beat of the measure. This note should be forceful at a *forte* level. Use a heavy beater and strike the bass drum in the center of the head.

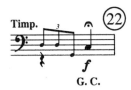

2. One Measure after Number 37:
   Rehearsal Number 37 (Jeu Du Rapt) begins a new section and this first measure is essentially a long tone. **I play the bass drum part slightly louder than the timpani at a *forte* level.** Gently muffle the drum with the leg while playing just off the center of the head. Carefully count and watch the conductor for accuracy.

3. One Measure after Number 45:
   The horn cue at rehearsal Number 44 is very clear for the entrance at the second measure after Number 45. The tuba and trombone have a pick-up note into the downbeat of the second measure after Number 45. **This bass drum note is quite explosive; so, strike it dead center of the head and with a lot of power.**

THE RITE OF SPRING by Igor Stravinsky
© Copyright 1912, 1921 by Hawkes & Son (London) Ltd.
Reprinted by permission of Boosey & Hawkes, Inc.

4. Number 47 to Number 48:

    There are a number of metric changes between Numbers 47 and 48 in which the eighth note remains constant. The 6/8 measures are conducted in two (with three eighth notes to the beat) and the 4/8 measures are also conducted in two (with two eighth notes per beat). **The bass drum has a solo entrance after a 3/4 measure. Use a very large hard beater and play this note very short (*secco*) at an *ff* dynamic (*sffz*).**

5. Number 49 to Number 53:

    All of the entrances between rehearsal Numbers 40 to 53 should resonate for two full beats. I suggest using a medium-heavy soft beater, preferably with an oblong-shaped head, to produce a dark tone with a weighty sound. Listen to the low strings and match their volume. **It also may help to strike the drum head off center with a "J" stroke to add more "thickness" to the sound.** In other words, do not strike the head straight on with a perpendicular motion. Use the weight of the arm when making the "J" stroke.

6. Number 53 to Number 54:

    Be aware that the timpani player has three grace notes leading into Number 53 and the subsequent measures. The timpanist can play them very open before the downbeat or more quickly into the downbeat. Discuss this with the timpanist before rehearsal. **These bass drum notes should be played closer to the center of the head in a very *marcato* manner.** Also, be aware that the 5/4 measure, four after Number 53, is sometimes broadened by adding a slight *ritard.*

    Editor's Note: The instruction in the score for the timpani part (*sonore*) and the "let-ring" signs were not added to the bass drum part; however, they are also important for the bass drum player. One word is which written in both parts, *assai,* and means "very." It indicates that these notes should be played very loud. *Sonore* means sonorous or resonant. It is important for the bass drum player to also have this in the part. The "let ring" signs should have been added to the bass drum part as well. *Sempre simile* means "always the same."

50

7. Number 55:

The section at rehearsal Number 54 moves very quickly (Vivo); so, be on your toes! **The four notes in the two measures after number 55 are best played as true quarter notes, muffling on beats two and four.** I suggest using a stroke with very little rebound. Use the weight of the arm when making the stroke and stay close to the head after striking.

8. Number 64 to Number 71:

There are many rhythmical layers to this section, building up to a frenzy, ultimately ending Part One. **The bass drum's role is to play three beats against four — creating a polyrhythmic effect.** Stravinsky adds the word *secco* to the part, asking for a short, dry sound. To obtain this effect, mute the playing head with the knee and the non-playing head with the left hand. Lock into the timpani's eighth notes at Number 67. The conductor will usually begin this section in four; then, at some point, change into two beats to the measure.

The tam tam enters at Number 68 with the same polyrhythmic effect; however, this entrance begins one and a half beats after the bass drum.

9. Number 70:

The section from Number 70 to 71 is difficult to follow. It is written in 6/4, but can be conducted in a number of ways. With 6 beats to the measure, it can be conducted in a subdivided two beats to the measure or a subdivided three beats to the measure. Either way, there should be a feeling of six beats.

Since the bass drum is usually placed right next to the timpani, I find it easiest to follow the timpani part. The accents are very strong in the timpani so the bass drum can simply play on the first and third beats of the measure. **The dynamic increases up to (at least) a *forte* at Number 70.** Be sure there is complete silence at Number 71.

The following illustrates the bass drum, guiro, and timpani parts at Number 70:

10. <u>Number 72:</u>

This section is the culmination of Part One and includes one of the most popular bass drum excerpts in orchestral literature.

Turn the bass drum to its horizontal position and play with two mallets (similar to the timpani). I find using small wood beaters, covered with a layer of chamois, works great for this part. I also suggest placing a large mute (small towel) on the head to produce a dry sound.

At number 72, the bass drum begins the Prestissimo in a very fast quarter-note pulse. Make a very abrupt *crescendo* in the first two measures, adding a separate *crescendo* on the tremolo of the third beat. **Execute this roll by using 5 strokes (place an accent on the final).** This allows the beginning and ending of the roll to be on the right (strong) hand. I have indicated the sticking below; but, it can easily be reversed for left-handed players.

All of the *sf* indications, from Number 72 to the downbeat of Number 74, are in an *ff* dynamic. Bear in mind that the *p* dynamic should be present and driving. Do not play too soft.

11. <u>Two Measures after Number 73:</u>

Take note: there should be a regular accent on the second beat of the second measure after Number 73 — this is not always indicated in the parts. This accent is not as strong as the three previous *sfp* accents.

12. <u>Number 74 to the End:</u>

It is important to pulse in a triplet feel from Number 74 to the end. To create this effect, use slight accents on each beat. **Do not overplay the accents — they should be "felt," not heard.** Continue to play at a healthy *p* in order to make an effective *p subito* at Number 75. Pace the *crescendo* evenly at Number 77. Play with one hand at Number 78 while placing one mallet down and picking up a harder, larger, and heavier (bomber) beater. Play the final quarter notes with the "bomber" beater, using as much *crescendo* as humanly possible!

Part Two

1. <u>Number 80 to Number 82:</u>
With the bass drum in the vertical position (upright), use a very soft pair of rolling mallets. Lean into the attack of the roll without producing an accent (*tenuto*); then, make the *diminuendo.*

2. <u>One Measure after Number 103:</u>
Stravinsky specifies the mallet choice here: *Colla bacc. di tamburo,* "with a snare drum stick." **I suggest using a large-headed wood timpani mallet.** A slappy, bright sound creates a nice effect which leads into the next section.

3. <u>Three Measures after Number 104:</u>
This measure (above) will, most likely, be conducted in three, creating a *hemiola* effect. The *poco f* is meant for each note — not just the first entrance. **Musically, it is appropriate to add a heavier accent on the final note of this measure and also to the downbeat at Number 105.**

4. <u>Number 111 to Number 112:</u>
Use a larger, heavier bass drum beater than the one for the previous sections, and treat these two notes like cannon shots.

5. <u>One Measure before Number 113 to Number 117</u>
Use a wood timpani mallet from one measure before Number 113 until Number 117, striking the head about ten inches from the rim. At Number 114, move closer to the edge of the drum head. Listen to the timpanist who also plays the eighth-note pattern.

Editor's Note: At one measure before Rehearsal Number 113, Stravinsky adds the instruction: *baguettes dures et sèches,* (hard sticks, and [play] very short and dry). For the bass drum he says: *bacc. di timp.,* (timpani sticks). As indicated at Number 5 (page 52), most timpani and bass drum players use wood sticks for this section.

6. <u>One Measure before Number 118:</u>
Some parts notate this measure as follows:

The correct notation is the same as one measure before Number 105:

7. <u>Number 122 to Number 128:</u>
All of the roll measures in this section are played with a *molto crescendo.* Most of the *crescendo* comes at the end of the roll. I suggest making a slight break before the single note that follows each roll.

8. <u>Number 128:</u>
I suggest using the single-headed bass drum for this section. The single head makes it easier to tune the Bb that Stravinsky specifies. Use a heavy, wood timpani stick or a small wood bass drum mallet. Strike the head as you would a timpani, about 4 to 5 inches from the rim. Keep in mind that the timpani and tambourine play on the off-beats. **I suggest playing these quarter notes as eighth notes and mute the drum head on the off-beats (where the timpani and tambourine play).**

Editor's Note: The French translation for the bass drum at Number 128 is: "with a wood stick, strike near the edge of the drum head to approximately produce a Bb."

9. Number 138 to Number 140:

This section is fairly maniacal with no discernable tonality; therefore, I suggest using the double-headed bass drum with a regular felt beater. Allow the notes to sustain with no muffling. **Hold a small wood beater in the non-playing hand for the quick switch at Number 139 (as indicated in the part). I suggest playing this section on the single-headed bass drum.** Muffle these notes in a similar manner to Number 128. At Number 140, return to the normal bass drum with the regular beater — again, without muffling. The shifts between the two bass drums, and the use of muffled notes verses sustained notes, are both very effective ideas.

10. One Measure before Number 173 to Number 174:

This mixed-meter section moves along quickly. The 2/16 and 3/16 measures are conducted in one beat to the measure, and the 2/8 measure is conducted in two beats to the measure. **The orchestra relies heavily on these four measures for accuracy; so, play them with a very sharp, biting accent.** The following shows the interaction between the bass drum and trombone parts:

11. Number 174 to Number 179:

Play the notes in this section close to the center of the head in order to produce the short, dry (secco) articulation asked for by the composer. Play the first two measures at a healthy *forte*; then, in the third measure, reduce the dynamic a bit, allowing the horns to be heard. The following illustrates the interaction between the bass drum, tam tam, and the first and second timpani parts:

12. <u>Number 180 to Number 181:</u>

Notice the rhythm modulation at rehearsal Number 180. The previous quarter note now equals an eighth note; therefore, the section at Number 180 is twice as slow. There is a fermata at the end of this bar; so, don't jump ahead!

13. <u>Number 186 to Number 190:</u>

Again, this mixed-meter section moves along quickly. **The 5/16 measures are conducted in two and are sub-divided as 2+3. The 2/16 and 3/16 measures are in one and the 2/8 measures are in two.**

The dynamic at Number 186 is only one *f*. The caveat being that the orchestration is not very thick; so don't overplay!

14. <u>Number 190 to Number 192:</u>

The timpani is the driving force in this final section of Part Two; therefore, support the timpani sound without dominating the tonality. The dynamic for the bass drum is an *f* at two measures before Number 192; however, I suggest reducing this to an *mf,* similar to the previous notes. The following is the interaction between the bass drum and timpani from Number 190 to 192:

56

15. <u>Number 192 to Number 197:</u>

All notes in this section are played at an *ff* dynamic — add an *sfffz* to each note. These notes are all in unison with the timpani. Again, support the timpani sound and strike the drum head directly in the center.

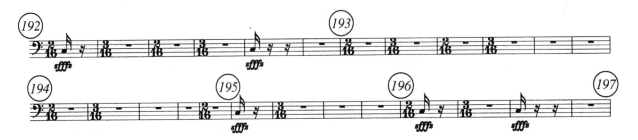

16. <u>Number 197 to Number 198:</u>

The downbeat of Number 197 should have an *sf* indication. **The bass drum entrance at the second measure after Number 197 is a mistake and should be omitted.** Also, add an *ff* on the third measure after Number 197; add accents to the notes beginning at three measures before Number 198; and an *sf* to the downbeat of Number 198. These notes are all in unison with the timpani.

17. <u>Three Measures before Number 199 to Number 202:</u>

Begin the third measure before Number 199 at a *meno f* dynamic to create a more effective *crescendo.* Play these notes as eighth notes without any muffling. **Along with the *crescendo,* add accents (as indicated below) to highlight the three-note rhythmic pattern in the orchestra.** Needless to say, the last note of the piece (Number 202) should be quite bombastic and harsh — after all, a poor girl did dance herself to death in this final scene!

SYMPHONY No. 3.

Gustav Mahler

Erste Abtheilung

No. 1.

Gr. Trommel

Mahler's *Symphony No. 3* has one of the most popular and exposed bass drum solos in all orchestral literature. A standard 36 x 20 inch bass drum, with calf heads on a hoop stand, works well and sounds best for this piece.

Before getting into the work, I would like to point out the differences between playing the bass drum in the vertical position as compared to the horizontal position. The bass drum played in the vertical position resonates more of the low overtones and sounds fuller. A bass drum played in the horizontal position (the bottom head facing directly toward the floor) loses these qualities. When both heads are put in motion and an object (such as the floor) blocks the sound waves, color and sound is sacrificed. Therefore, keep the drum in the vertical position (or slightly tilted) whenever possible. It may cause the execution of some excerpts to be more problematic, but with proper mallets, correct muting, careful choice of the beating spot, and most of all, outstanding technique, the final result will be more satisfactory than when the bass drum is in the horizontal position. **I play the entire Symphony with the bass drum in the vertical or near vertical position.**

1. Three Measures before Number 1:
   The tempo indication above this measure (Zurückhaltend) indicates that the tempo will pull back. **Place an emphasis (*tenuto*) on the first and third measures before Number 1 to balance with the contra bassoon and low brass.**

2. Number 1:

Mahler asks for *mit 2 Schwammschlägeln* (with 2 sponge mallets) at rehearsal Number 1. **For our purposes, felt-headed mallets will achieve a beautiful roll and decent articulation for the grace notes before Number 2.** The use of a double-headed mallet is also a possibility (one end made of soft felt and the other a harder and firmer covering). A mallet with a smaller but heavier core, firmly wrapped with German felt, works well.

When starting the roll, play the first two strokes close together but with a slight accent (*tenuto*). Then, taper the roll speed by slowing up the strokes — like a timpani roll. The beating spot should be between the center and the edge of the head. Find the ideal beating spot on your particular bass drum. **Play very quietly and do not muffle the head.**

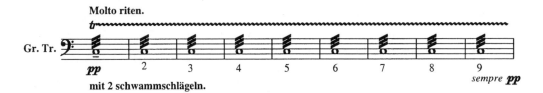

3. Four Measures before Number 2:

The solo at four measures before Number 2 is dark in nature, requiring great technique. **For the first measure, play near the center of the head and only use one hand.** Muffle the drum head a bit with the leg to produce a clear articulation. Notice the *Nicht schleppen* indication (do not drag) at this point. **I suggest directing the first four eighth notes towards the middle of the measure in pace and dynamics, and just the opposite for the triplets.** Do this with great subtlety. The roll in the second bar of this four-measure solo should not have a strong accent on the attack. It should sound dark and resonant; so, move closer to the edge of the drum head and use the same subtle attack as at Number 1.

The next two measures need an explanation. Mahler wrote the grace notes for the bass drum as a 4-stroke ruff; however, when the brass instruments enter at Number 2, their figure is written as a sixteenth-note triplet. **The bass drum and trombone figures should be played identically.** The trombones delay the entrance a bit so the figure moves quickly into the downbeat. In order to obtain the same effect, the bass drum player needs to slow down the three grace notes. These grace notes should also have the subtle feeling of a *crescendo* into the main note.

Mahler also indicates that the section at Number 2 should be played *Schwer und dumpft*, (heavy and muted). Be sure to muffle the drum head by pressing into the head with as much of the leg as possible after each quarter note. Play directly into the center of the drumhead using two mallets for the grace notes. **Play with a firm grip (*staccato*) and dig into the head within the** *pp* **dynamic to produce as much articulation as possible.**

4. Four Measures after Number 3 and One Measure before Number 4:
   Even though the dynamic says *sempre pp,* "always very soft," increase the dynamic in these two measures as indicated to adjust the balance with the orchestra:

5. Nine Measures before Number 5:
   This *ff* entrance should blend with the strings and brass instruments. **Allow the note to ring for a full two beats and then gently muffle to create a "dying-away" effect.**

6. Six Measures before Number 11:
   All the same comments apply here as for the entrance before Number 2; however, the tempo can be slightly faster. Hold the roll at three measures before Number 11 for the full four beats. **Since the following grace notes continue to come before the downbeat, there will be small gap between the roll and two measures before Number 11.**

7. Number 12:

    The dynamic for the bass drum at three measures after Number 12 is *f*; however, the rest of the orchestra plays *ff*. The timpani has an *sf* on this note and also needs a similar strong attack. The bass drum note should sustain for the entire measure. For accuracy, listen to the three grace notes into the downbeat of the third measure after Number 12 in the clarinets. The entire orchestra enters with the bass drum at three measures after Number 12. The following is an edited version of the bass drum part:

8. Eight Measures before Number 13:

    Play the eight measures before Number 13 in a very soft dynamic even though this is a solo for the percussion section. The fourth measure before Number 13 should be played a bit louder, and the final note, one measure before Number 13, a bit softer than the previous measure. **Muffle these two final notes so they do not resonate.**

Editor's Note: The German instruction six measures before Number 13 translates as: "Cymbal attached (to the bass drum) but played by two musicians." *Gr. Tr. allein* means "Bass drum alone." *Lange* means "long."

9. Number 13 to Number 16:

Mahler now writes a sixteenth-note triplet in place of the three grace notes. He adds the instruction: *Die Triolen immer schnell (als Vorschläge) ausgeführt* (The triplets are always executed quickly [like the grace notes]). **Basically, the three grace notes and the triplet-sixteenth rhythms are played the same.**

The 3/2 measures are usually conducted in three; so the tempo moves a bit faster. **This section features a trombone solo and is quite *rubato*.** The trombone and bass drum parts are as follows:

10. Seven Measures before Number 17:

Be sure to notice the *accel.* indication over the trombone cue in this measure. **Only make a *poco dim.* in this measure to be sure all sixteenth notes can be heard.** I have added *staccato* markings to the sixteenth notes to add clarity to the rhythm and an *fp* on the downbeat of the roll. I perform this measure as follows:

The roll continues for four more measures in some editions:

11. Number 27:

Increase the dynamic a bit at Number 27. **Be careful not to cover the horns during the *crescendo* in the tenth measure after Number 27.**

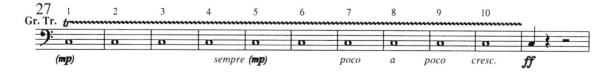

12. <u>Seven Measures before Number 29:</u>
   Since these measures may broaden a bit (*Zurückhaltend*) during this section, keep an eye on the conductor. Also, add a slight attack to the beginning of the roll.

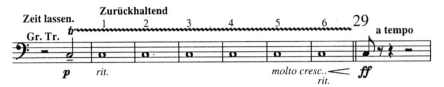

13. <u>Nine Measures before Number 33:</u>
   There is an *accel.* one measure before this entrance; so, even though the rhythms become slower, the tempo is getting faster until four measures before Number 33 where there is another *Zurückhalten* (holding back).

   The first entrance has a *dim.* and a hairpin *decrescendo*; however, continue at the *f* dynamic for the entire measure and then make a *subito mf* on the second bar. The third measure should be played at an *mp* dynamic with a *dim.* in the fourth measure to a *p*; however, the solo continues so do not get too soft during the *dim.* into two measures before Number 33. The *dim.* must continue until Number 33. The following is my edited version of these measures:

14. <u>One Measure before Number 49:</u>
   The German phrase *Von einem geschlagen.* means "for one player." **The bass drummer, using a cymbal attached to the shell of the bass drum, now plays both the bass drum and cymbal parts.** The entrance, one measure before Number 49, is marked *p* (in some parts), but it should be played *f* and in a raucous manner.

15. <u>Six Measures before Number 52:</u>
   At six measures before Number 52 there is a *più mosso* indication — be ready to increase the tempo. By this point, the conductor will be conducting in two beats to the measure. Even though this section is very raucous and chaotic, don't get too carried away with the dynamics. The original dynamic begins at an *mf*; however, I suggest playing at an *f* level.

   Three measures before Number 53 is a mistake. The bass drum does not play during this measure; the first and fourth measures before Number 53 should be identical. The dynamics in the score and part conflict between four measures after Number 51 to Number 53. I believe the dynamics for this section to be as follows:

16. Three Measures before Number 56 to Number 57:
Do not muffle the three notes before Number 56. They should all ring through the rests. The solo and grace notes, at four measures before Number 57, should be in the same style as previously discussed. This solo is now played at a *p* instead of the *pp* as before. Exaggerate the *diminuendo* one measure before Number 57.

17. One Measure before Number 58 to Number 60:
The trombone solo begins at this point; therefore, the tempo becomes more *rubato* as before.

18. Nine Measures before Number 63:
The bass drum/cymbal attachment part for this section is very exposed with only the bass and celli playing. **Treat all notes as half notes — do not muffle.**

19. Number 70:
The German instructions at Number 70, *Becken an der grossen Trommel befestigt, aber ohne grosse trommel.* means "(Play) the attached cymbal on the bass drum, but without the bass drum." **This part is played by the bass drummer.** Follow the snare drum part for accuracy.

20. Three Measures before Number 73:
Be aware, at this point, there may be a holding back during the *crescendo*.

21. <u>Number 74:</u>

Watch the conductor carefully at Number 74 because the tempo becomes slower during these measures. *Zeit lassen* means to "allow time."

No. 3.

1. <u>Eight Measures before Number 17:</u>

Let these notes ring and play them with great warmth and depth within the *p* dynamic. The German term *deutlich* means "clear and distinct."

2. <u>One Measure before Number 30:</u>

This entrance is very soft but, remember, it is a solo. **I suggest adding the hairpin *crescendo* and *diminuendo* for expression.**

No. 6.

1. <u>Two Measures before Number 19:</u>

The note following the roll must be very carefully placed together with the timpani entrance. **Since this entrance is delayed, watch the conductor and listen to the timpani.**

The tempo marking at Number 18, *Etwas breiter als vorher,* means "Somewhat slower as before."

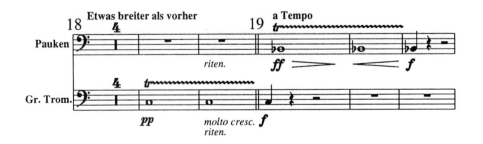

2. Five Measures after Number 28:
    The trumpet and violins have a quintuplet leading into the sixth measure of
    Number 28. **Listening to these instruments helps to place the note accurately
    following the roll.**

3. One Measure before Number 31:
    Muffle the bass drum immediately before Number 31. **There is a comma (*pause)*
    immediately before Number 31.** The German instruction, *Wieder etwas
    zurückhaltend.,* means "Again, somewhat holding back."

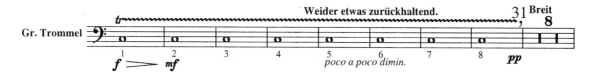

CAPRICCIO ESPAGNOL
N. Rimsky Korsakow

Castagnetti

V. Fandango asturiano

Orchestral castanet playing is best executed with handle or machine castanets. There are two types of handle castanets: those activated by shaking the castanets against a board; and those activated by the castanets striking each other against the upper part of the leg.

The Spanish *Fandango* is a dance for guitar and castanets. The castanets play a prominent role in this orchestral setting. The *Fandango* is preceded by the *Canto gitano* without a break — or in musical terms, an *attacca*.

1. Opening Twelve Measures:
   Phrase each measure by adding an accent on the first beat. Strike both castanets together on the third beat by adding a flam. This adds character to the part. The following is my edited version of the opening section:

2. Twelve Measures before Letter T:
   The dynamic level at Letter T is only one *p*. However, the character of the castanets throughout the movement is soloistic; so, only consider the dynamics for balance purposes. This instrument provides flair and color to the music.

   The *trill* indication is meant to emulate extremely fast single strokes played by dancers using finger castanets. **By slightly pressing the top of the castanet with the index finger, you can achieve two beats per wrist stroke, producing these rapid bounces.** With practice, the rolls can be executed at all dynamic levels.

   There is a discrepancy in the part at four measures before Letter T. The bracketed measures (below) show the accurate notation:

3. Two Measures before Letter U:
   To create a nice effect, decrease the dynamic level at two measures before Letter U; then, make a *crescendo* into Letter U.

4. <u>Letter V to the Coda</u>:

In some scores, Letter V is notated with two slashes as abbreviated sixteenth notes; other parts have three slashes, indicating a roll. Either version works; however, **I suggest using sixteenths at Letter V and then switching to the roll at Letter W for the *ff* dynamic.** Also, don't forget to add the flam effect on the third beat from Letter W to the Coda.

5. <u>Coda</u>:

Keep an eye on the conductor during the Coda since the tempo may increase before the Presto. Again, feel free to add a flam to the first quarter note of the Coda.

6. <u>Coda to the End</u>:

The notation in the score and parts differ in this section between sixteenth notes and rolls. **I suggest playing sixteenth notes with the exception of rolling the ninth and second measures before Letter Y.** Looking at the woodwind and brass parts, the rolls in the castanet part line up with the syncopated quarter notes in the winds. The sixteenth notes line up with the eighth-note rhythms.

CUBAN OVERTURE
George Gershwin

Maracas

The use of maracas do not find their way into orchestral music very often. However, in *Cuban Overture* by George Gershwin, it is a prominent and effectively-used instrument. I find the Venezuelan maracas, with a very hard shell (almost like the hardness of a coconut shell) and large beads work great. Those with leather shells do not project the sound and are not bright enough for this piece. Take note that each maraca has a different pitch (high and low) and, Gershwin, having spent some time in Cuba, was savvy to this information. He specified high and low sounds, notating the pitches on two staff lines.

The technique for this piece is best achieved by holding the maracas at a 45 degree angle to the ground. Use a quick, up-down stroke to produce the dotted eighth and sixteenth rhythm (notated as follows):

U = upstroke
D = downstroke

The right hand holds the higher-pitched maraca; the left hand holds the lower-pitched maraca.

Another method for playing this part is to alternate all the rhythms and ignore the upper and lower sounds.

1. Number 3 and Number 5:
   With the exception of the last two measures, only two rhythms are used throughout the piece:

   The measure at Number 5 adds a flourish on the second beat. I emphasize the entire second beat so as to increase the rhythm's color. The actual rhythm of the dotted sixteenth and thirty-second notes do not have to be exact. **The rhythm is actually closer to straight sixteenth notes (as shown below):**

2. Number 3 to Seven Measures after Number 4:
   This is conducted in *"alle breve"* or two beats to the measure. Play confidently and blend with the rest of the percussion section. **Always keep an ear on the clave rhythm, the grounding rhythm throughout the piece.**

Cuban sticks (Claves)

Maracas

CUBAN OVERTURE By GEORGE GERSHWIN© 1933 (Renewed) WB MUSIC CORP.
GERSHWIN® and GEORGE GERSHWIN® are registered trademarks of Gershwin Enterprises
All Rights Reserved   Used by Permission

3. <u>Number 5 to Number 7:</u>
    This section has a flourish on the second beat. **If not indicated, the dynamic level is**
    mf. The last measure in this section (two measures before Number 7) is as follows,
    with the final note in the measure on the low maraca:

4. <u>Five Measures before Number 9:</u>
    Starting at *mf,* make a *diminuendo* in measures two and three to an *mp,* ending at *p* at
    Number 9.

5. <u>Two Measures before Number 10:</u>
    Add a *crescendo* at two measures before Number 10 to an *mf* to accommodate
    the *crescendo* in the orchestra.

6. <u>Number 12 to Number 14:</u>
    - **Even though this section is marked *pp*, play it with prominence so the entire**
      orchestra can hear it. It is also acceptable to include the second beat flourish at
      seven measures after Number 13.

7. <u>Number 17 to Number 18:</u>
Do not take the *pp* dynamic literally. **Adjust to the orchestral sound and do not make a *diminuendo* into the dynamic change at Number 18.**

8. <u>One Measure before Number 26:</u>
The pickup notes into Number 26 immediately begin the Allegretto ritmico tempo. They are a bit quicker than the previous Sostenuto tempo at Number 19. **There is a *subito p* at the Allegro ritmico on the second beat (not in the part); however, this occurs over a beat or two. Again, do not take this too literally.**

9. <u>Six Measures before Number 28:</u>
Follow the general direction of the orchestra throughout this section without compromising the maraca rhythm. Again, do not take the dynamics too literally. Therefore, mimic the dynamic changes here by reducing the sound a bit on the seventh measure after Number 27, creating the feel of a *crescendo* back to the previous level at Number 28.

10. <u>Three Measures before Number 29:</u>
Increase the dynamic three measures before Number 29 to balance with the trumpets; then, reduce the dynamic at Number 29 to balance with the woodwinds. Adjust the dynamics once again on the third and fourth measures after Number 29.

11. <u>Two Measures before Number 31 to Four Measures before Number 33:</u>
Although it is not written in the parts, the orchestra begins a *crescendo* two measures before Number 31. This continues until four measures before Number 33; so, pace the *crescendo* during this section.

12. <u>Number 34:</u>
As indicated in the tempo marking at Number 34 (*Grandly, only slightly slower*), the tempo broadens here; so be prepared!

13. <u>Number 35:</u>
Notice the Animato tempo indication at Number 35. This is an immediately faster tempo change. It may constantly move forward until the end. **Also, increase the dynamic at this point.**

14. <u>Three Measures from the End:</u>
Use the following "sticking" in the third measure from the end:

15. <u>Final Two Measures:</u>
The final two measures are omitted in the maraca part. I suggest playing double stops and using the following sticking:

SYMPHONIC DANCES FROM "WEST SIDE STORY"
Leonard Bernstein

A large battery of percussion instruments is used in Leonard Bernstein's *West Side Story*; but, the focus of this analysis will be on the tom tom part. Depending on the orchestra's tradition, much of the tom tom part is played on drum set.

The part is notated for four pitched drums; but, it does not mean actual pitches. Bernstein simply separates each drum from low to high — approximately an interval of a third apart. I use small drums: 8, 10, 12, and 13 inches, played with a small-headed stick (5B).

1. Measures 48 to 60:
   The first solo entrance of the tom toms begins at measure 48. The previous tenor drum part is played on the drum set. **To eliminate any crossing, I use the following set up:**

   The tom tom entrance at measure 48 is a solo with no orchestral accompaniment. Play with confidence and maintain a solid presence even though the dynamic is *p*. Do not make any *crescendo* during this passage. The trombone plays a *sfz* note on the pick-up note; so, make sure the first note of the solo can be heard. **To avoid any cross sticking, start all the triplets with the right hand and use alternating strokes.**

   Note: The bassoon and trombones come in on the downbeat of measure 54. **To help the passage "swing," I phrase measures 52 to 60 in the following fashion:**

2. Measures 96 to 99:
   Do not speed up during the *crescendo*. I suggest the following sticking for measures 95 to 99:

SYMPHONIC DANCES FROM WEST SIDE STORY by Leonard Bernstein
© Copyright 1967 by Amberson Holdings LLC. Copyright Renewed.
Leonard Bernstein Music Publishing LLC, Publisher
Boosey & Hawkes, Inc., Sole Agent
Reprinted by permission

3. Measures 132 and 133:

The pulse remains the same as in the previous measures with the dotted-quarter note equaling the quarter note. **Come in strong with an *ff* dynamic and focus on the pick-up note in the timpani for an accurate entrance.**

4. Measures 133 to 138:

Maintain a steady tempo. **Phrase as indicated below. These articulations should be subtle — do not overplay.** A *quasi crescendo* is implied in measures 135 and 136. Measure 138 is marked as *fff* and must be very strong.

5. Measures 177 to 254:

The tom tom part from measures 177 to 254 can be played either by the four concert toms (as written) or on the drum set.

6. Measures 381 to 384:

This section should be played on concert tom toms. I suggest using a pair of snare drum sticks with the tips covered with a piece of moleskin to soften the texture. **Play this section in two-measure phrases and also pulse the beamed-note groupings.**

Editor's Note: The original manuscript for *West Side Story* shows the above section played on three concert toms. The latter engraved version has this section arranged for four concert toms (shown on page 73).

7. <u>Measure 394:</u>
   I suggest beginning the dynamic at an *mf* and making a strong *crescendo* into a *sfz*. **Do not let the drums ring into the G.P.** I suggest using snare drum sticks for this measure.

8. <u>Measures 466 to the End:</u>
   This section can be played entirely on drum set or spilt between concert toms as follows:

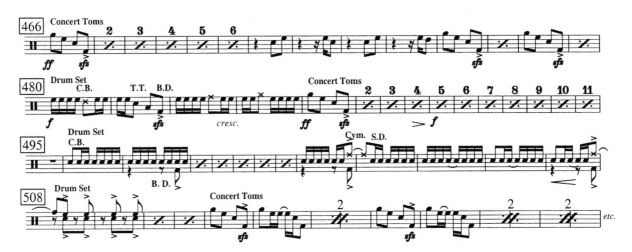

THE ROSE LAKE
Michael Tippett
Roto-Toms

Michael Tippett composed *The Rose Lake* in 1995 for the Boston Symphony. Although it is not necessarily an audition piece or a work that appears often in the orchestral repertoire, it is a work of particular note for percussionists. Inevitably, I will receive a phone call from the unlucky recipient of this part who asks: "How do I do it?" Hopefully, this analysis will answer all questions.

The Rose Lake uses a large battery of percussion, including 40 roto-toms which I will discuss here. The actual performance is straightforward, but the set up is complicated.

In the beginning, two percussionists play all 40 roto-toms; then, only one player is used for the remainder of the work. **Although Tippett originally suggested two players for the entire piece, I find this too difficult to execute with evenness and continuity.** Tippett says: "Either the percussionist will have to leave out some of the notes or should have extremely long arms!" Neither criterion is necessary with my system.

The work is written in six sections, without a break and roto-toms are used in five of the sections. The key to performing this piece with one player is the roto-tom configuration. **After the first section, the player must physically move all the drums for the remainder of the work.** Fortunately, there is plenty of time to do this; but, since it is such a huge setup; it has to be done as discretely as possible.

The roto-tom sizes vary from 6 to 18 inches. The various drums fit onto racks. Each rack is 33 inches long. There are also three shorter racks attached at either a 90 or 45-degree angle. The pitched roto-toms are set up like a piano keyboard. There are 10 racks in total. Racks 1 through 7 are 33 inches long and contain 36 roto-toms of varying sizes. The remaining racks have different lengths. Rack A is 12 inches long and contains two roto-toms. Racks B and C are 6 inches long and each rack contains one roto-tom with a specific pitch (depending where it is used). **A diagram of all ten racks, with their respective bar sizes, the amount and sizes of drums, pitches, and bar angles for the accidentals, are notated below:**

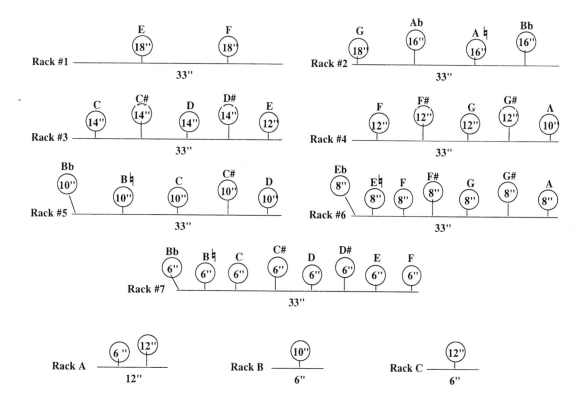

The playing area and tuning of the roto-toms require some explanation. The correct beating area is similar to the timpani — somewhere between the rim and center of the head. This produces the clearest and most resonant tone. Each drum has a different number of lugs, depending on size, and the roto-tom can only obtain a clear, discernable pitch when the lugs are at equal tension. **It takes a considerable amount of time to tune each drum and if a new head is used, this process may need to be repeated over a few days.**

In addition to changing the set-up, I also change specific notes to eliminate awkward sticking or crossing. When a note has been changed from its original pitch, it is circled on the diagram.

Rack 5, in its original form, looks like this:

Rack #5

When a note is changed from its original pitch, it will be circled:

Rack #5

1. <u>Number 1 to Number 7:</u>
   The set-up for this section uses Racks 3 to 7 and Rack B. The pitch for Rack B should be set to an A below middle C. Place Rack B between Racks 5 and 6. The C natural on Rack 5 needs to be changed to a C# for this section.

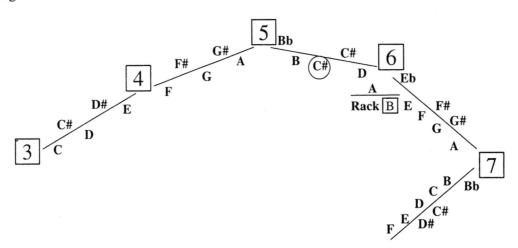

The roto-toms should all be in a semi-circle at one height. Make sure the circle is large enough to accommodate two players. For convenience purposes, I have indicated the sticking on each part. The accidentals carry throughout the entire measure. Rack 5 will have two C sharps. Either of the C#s can be used; however, I use the altered C# throughout this entire section. Rack B is only used at Number 5 and two measures after Number 5, when the low A appears. Player Two has a B natural immediately before the A natural for Player One; so, using Rack B helps avoid a collision between them.

I suggest Player One use a round, beaded snare drum stick with a thin covering such as mole skin. Player Two should use a small-headed, hard-felt timpani mallet. **Whatever sticks or mallets are used, be sure the pitch and articulation of the roto-toms are audible at a quiet dynamic.**

The first harp begins this section and the second harp enters at measure three. When starting at measure five, try to lock onto the harp's rhythm. The rhythmic pattern is basically sixteenth-note triplets. Remain at the *pp* level through two measures after Number 4. **At Number 5, the orchestration is a bit thicker; so, increase the dynamic level and follow the indicated changes.**

2. <u>Measures 39 to 48 and 144 to 151:</u>
   From this point until the end, the roto-tom part should be played by one player. This bubbly section also appears in Section Two and then returns in Section 5. The roto-tom setup is now changed to the follow arrangement:

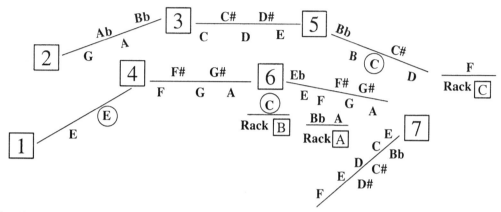

Notice Racks 1, 4, 6, 7, B and A should be at the same height (lower level) as the previous section. Racks 2, 3, 5 and C should be behind the front row and higher. Also, note the pitch change on Rack 1. The C# on Rack 5 must now return to C natural. Rack A should be tuned to Bb above middle C (on the left) and A below middle C (on the right). Rack B should be tuned to middle C and Rack C should be tuned to F below middle C. With this set-up and sticking, performance at this fast tempo is possible. **Needless to say, this section will probably have to be memorized.** Sticking is notated on the part whenever Racks A, B, and C are used.

The actual part is not as complicated as it seems. There is plenty of time from Number 7 to measure 39 to reset the roto-toms. **It is not necessary to count during the rests because of the obvious cue before the entrance.** Section Two starts very slowly in the horns. At Number 26 below, an obvious change to a faster tempo occurs in the winds, followed by a few measures with the harps and keyboard percussion.

The previous measures happen three times. The trumpets and trombones enter with a series of *fp* long tones for six measures, at which time the orchestra will arrive at Number 39. I have always been able to complete my setup well before Number 39. **The roto-tom entrance is quite prominent; so, enter as a soloist with a strong presence.** Follow the phrasing of the horns and make a big *crescendo*, as written, in the sixth measure. This repeats nine bars later.

The section at Number 47 is an awkward three measures. It involves Racks A, B, and C. The sticking I use is listed below. These measures are quite exposed (only the violas play as an accompaniment). Do not be tempted to rush the 5/8 measure (a slower section immediately follows these measures). It helps to slightly pulse each eighth count from the pick-up notes before the 5/8 measure — do not make any feeling of a *crescendo* — the violas are in the low register of their instrument. **I find these three measure to be the most difficult in the entire work.**

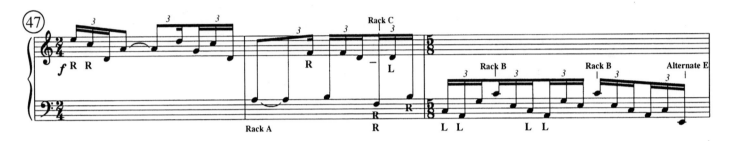

3. Number 96 to Four Measures after Number 103:
   There is plenty of time from the previous section to Number 96. All that needs to be accomplished is to change seven pitches. **The Racks will not have to be moved for the rest of the piece.** The pitch changes are notated below:

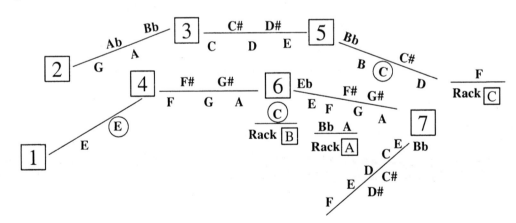

Since the normal order of pitches are from low to high, it's easy to become confused with the new pitch changes. **These changes are necessary in order to avoid long, awkward reaches and once the hands become familiar with the motions, playing this section becomes quite easy.**

The section between Number 96 and 103 is very *mysterioso* and is often accompanied by only one other instrument. Roto-toms have the lead voice, colored by the harp and clarinet. I use a small, light timpani mallet which produces clarity and also a nice warm tone. Play all rolls as single strokes — like a timpani roll. **Do not overplay the accents in this section; just add a bit of extra weight to the stroke and fall back.**

4. <u>Number 144 to Number 155:</u>

   This section is an exact repeat of Number 39 to Number 46; so, re-tune the pitches to the previous set-up.

5. <u>Number 163 to Number 168:</u>

   This is a variation of the opening measures at Number 1. **As with other roto-tom sections, it is very exposed — only a marimba plays along with the roto-toms.** Everything is played with double strokes unless otherwise indicated. I have also indicated where Racks A and B are used. There are three pitch changes (circled) for this section as notated below:

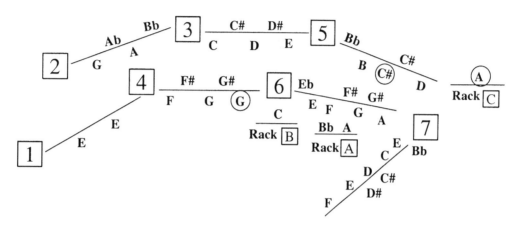

Take note that the marimba always begins one beat ahead of the roto-tom entrance at Number 163; so, lock onto this rhythm for accuracy. Start the *crescendi* a bit earlier every time the figure returns. Below are examples at Number 163 and 164.

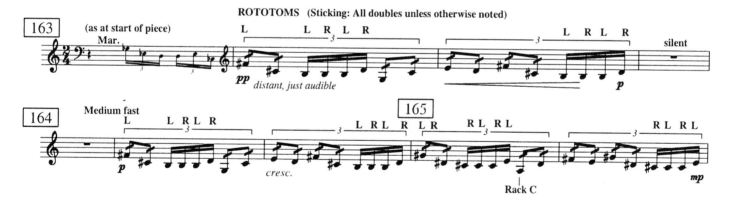

6. <u>Conclusion:</u>

   The roto-tom part requires quite a bit of preparation; however, if one is diligent in following the guidelines I have set forth, I believe the end result will be quite rewarding and impressive.

૭૦જી

About the Author

Timothy E. Genis, current Principal Timpanist of the Boston Symphony, also served as Assistant Timpanist/Percussionist from 1993–2003. He is Head of the Percussion Department at Boston University, Boston University Tanglewood Institute, and Section Leader for the Tanglewood Music Center. Tim was previously the Principal Percussionist of the Honolulu Symphony and Assistant Timpanist with the Hong Kong Philharmonic. He has also performed with the Vienna Philharmonic, New York Philharmonic, Radio City Orchestra, and Rochester Philharmonic.

Mr. Genis graduated from The Juilliard School and has studied with Roland Kohloff, Buster Bailey, Chris Lamb, Joe Morello, John Beck, and Anthony Cirone. As an avid clinician, he has given Master Classes throughout North America, Europe, and Asia. Tim has also developed a line of timpani and snare drum sticks currently marketed by Vic Firth, Inc.